Step into the...

Arctic World

Jen Green

Consultant: Cherry Alexander

HERMES
HOUSE

First published in 2000 by Hermes House

© Anness Publishing Limited 2000

Hermes House is an imprint of Anness
Publishing Limited, Hermes House, 88–89
Blackfriars Road, London SE1 8HA.

A CIP catalogue record for this book is
available from the British Library

Publisher: Joanna Lorenz
Managing Editor, Children's Books:
Gilly Cameron Cooper
Senior Editor: Nicole Pearson
Editor: Leon Gray
Designer: Caroline Reeves
Illustration: Vanessa Card, Stuart Carter,
Shane Marsh
Special Photography: John Freeman
Stylist: Konika Shankar

Anness Publishing would like to thank the following
children for modelling for this book: Josie Ainscough,
Laurence Ainscough, Harriet Bartholomew, Carissa
Cork, Louan Harrison, Stephanie Harvey, John
Jlitakryan, Muhammed Laher, Monilola Majekodunmi,
Salem Miah, Ben Rodden, Carl Simpson.

PICTURE CREDITS
b=bottom, t=top, c=centre, l=left, r=right
Bryan & Cherry Alexander: 4cl; 5c, cl & tl; 8c & tl; 9tl,
cl & cr; 10bl & tl; 11tl, tr, cl & cr; 12 tl, bl & br; 13cr,
bl & br; 14 tl & cl; 15tr & cl; 16bl; 17c; 18tl; 19tl &
tr; 20c & tl; 21cl & cr; 22cl & cr; 23tr & cl; 24c; 25tl
& tr; 27ct & cr; 28cr; 29cl; 30tl, cl & cr; 31tr; 32cl;
33cl; 35tl; 36tl; 38tl & bl; 39tr, cr, bl, & br; 41tl; 42tr;
43tr; 44tl; 45c & tl; 46c & tl; 47cl, cl & tr; 48tl; 49tr,
cl & cr; 50cr; 51tl & tr; 52cl; 54tl & br; 55l & tr; 56bl;
57tl, tr & br; 58bl; 59tr, bl & br; 60tl & bl; 61 tr & br.
The Art Archive: 40tl. BBC Natural History Unit /Jose
Schell: 21tr. Bridgeman Art Library: 18cr; 37t; 40b;
41cl. Camera Press: 52tl. Corbis Images: 17tl; 27cl;
29cr & tl; 36br; 37b; 43b; 44cr; 45cl; 51cl; 54cl; 55cr.
Mary Evans Picture Library: 4tl; 23tl; 27tr; 28tl; 33tr;
41bl; 42b; 43tl; 48cr. Robert Harding / W. Herbert:
31cl. Oxford Scientific Films / Doug Allen:31tl; /
Richard & Julia Kemp: 24tl & 26tl; / Malcolm Penny:
61tl. Planet Earth: 29tr; 58tl; / Bryan & Cherry
Alexander: 16tl; / John Eastcott: 21tl & 39tl; / F. Jack
Jackson: 26cl; 32tl & 33tl; / Louise Murray: 55bl; /
Tom Walker: 34tl & 35tr. Ann Ronan: 43cl. Scanpix
Norge: 61cl. Science & Society: 42cr. Scott Polar
Research Institute: 50tl; 53cl; 56tl; 57cl. Tony Stone
Images / James Balog 17tr; / P H Cornutt: 19cl; /
Natalie Fobes: 13tl; / Derke-O'Hara: 25cl; / George
Lepp: 11br.

Printed and bound in Singapore
10 9 8 7 6 5 4 3 2 1

CONTENTS

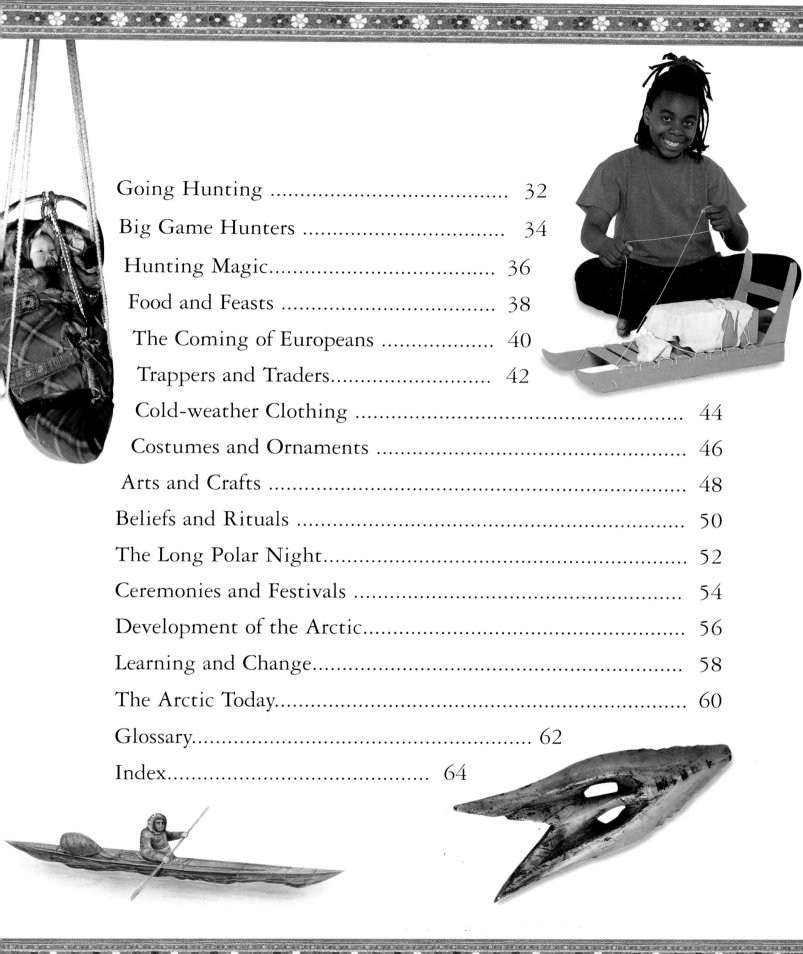

An Ancient History

EARLY PORTRAIT
This portrait of three Arctic hunters was painted in the 1800s by one of the first European explorers to visit the Arctic. Drawings made by early European explorers, along with other records they collected, are a good source of information about the history of the region.

THE ARCTIC is one of the wildest, harshest places on Earth. Arctic winters are long, dark and bitterly cold. A thick layer of ice and snow blankets the region for much of the year. Today, people from developed countries can survive in the Arctic with the help of the latest technologies, such as modern homes, petrol-driven snowmobiles and clothes made from warm man-made fibres. Yet the original Arctic inhabitants thrived in this icy world for thousands of years. They did not have any of these modern aids to help them.

Arctic peoples used the natural world around them to survive. Slain animals provided food, skins for clothes and shelter and bones for tools and weapons. Although early Arctic peoples left no written records behind them, archaeologists can piece together the history of these people from finds such as tools and the remains of old buildings. The modern descendants of these early residents continue to carry on some of the traditional ways of Arctic living.

TRADITIONAL SKILLS
A girl from Arctic Russia learns to soften reindeer skins, using a method that has been used by her ancestors for thousands of years. Ancient Arctic peoples developed a way of life that was so successful that it has changed very little over the generations.

TIMELINE 10,000BC–AD1600

Humans have lived in the Arctic region for thousands of years. The huge periods of time involved, and the lack of written records, mean that the dates given to some of the earlier events are only approximate.

10,000BC and earlier Groups of people in Arctic Russia and Scandinavia live a nomadic life, following huge herds of reindeer that they hunt for food.

10,000BC During the last Ice Age, nomadic peoples move into North America from Siberia, travelling across a bridge of dry land that linked the two landmasses.

Small Tool People harpoon used to hunt sea mammals

3000–1000BC The Small Tool People live on the shores of the Bering Strait. Later they move east into Arctic Canada and Greenland. They use tools, such as needles to make clothes, and harpoons to hunt food.

1000BC–AD1000 The Dorset People dominate the North American Arctic. They use sea *kayaks* to hunt sea mammals, such as seals and walruses. The Dorset People live a nomadic life during the summer months, travelling in small groups and living in skin-covered tents.

Dorset culture hunter in his kayak

10,000BC   5000BC   1000BC

ANCIENT SITES

Archaeologists unearth the remains of a prehistoric house in the Canadian Arctic. Excavations of these early settlements reveal tools, weapons and other important objects. This information can tell archaeologists a lot about the lives of early Arctic people.

TOOLS AND WEAPONS

This harpoon point was carved from a walrus tusk. In ancient times, Arctic people were skilled at many crafts. Numerous tools and weapons were shaped from the bones of slain animals.

KEEPING TRADITIONS ALIVE

Inuit children get ready for a traditional feast of seabird meat, prepared according to an age-old recipe. Feasts and festivals such as these help to keep ancient Arctic traditions alive, preserving them for future generations of Inuit to enjoy.

FROZEN WORLD

The Arctic region lies at the far north of our planet. Its limit is the Arctic Circle, an imaginary line encircling the Earth at a latitude of 66 degrees north. Much of the Arctic region is a vast, frozen ocean, surrounded by the northernmost parts of Asia, Europe, North America and Greenland. All areas inside the Arctic Circle experience at least one day each year when the Sun shines all day and night, and at least one day when the Sun never rises.

---

knife of Dorset origin

AD1–AD1000 In winter, the Dorset people live in snow-house communities and use knives and clubs to kill seals at their breathing holes on the sea ice. During the later Dorset period, they develop artistic abilities. Many of the objects they make are used for magic, such as wooden masks. Around AD1000 the climatic becomes warmer, which leads to the extinction of many of the Dorset people.

AD983 Viking warrior Erik the Red establishes a colony in Greenland.

Viking colony established in Greenland

AD1000–1600 The Thule People take over from the Dorset People. They live in stone and turf huts. They use *kayaks* and *umiaks* to hunt bowhead whales, and kill land animals, such as reindeer and musk oxen.

AD1570 onwards European sailors begin to explore the coast of Arctic Canada and also the seas north of Siberia. They come in search of whale oil, furs and wealth, and to find new sea routes to Asia.

Thule People continue to prosper until 1600

AD1000   AD1500   AD1600

The Arctic World

THE ICY WORLD of the Arctic holds traces of some very ancient civilizations. Indeed, archaeologists have found tools and weapons dating back to around 20,000BC. In prehistoric times, Arctic Russia and Scandinavia were inhabited by nomadic (wandering) peoples. They followed huge herds of reindeer, hunting the animals for their meat and fur. During the last Ice Age, more than 12,000 years ago, some of these nomads travelled from Asia to North America, crossing a bridge of land that once linked the two continents. Some settled in Arctic North America, while others moved to the warmer climate of the south.

Around 3000BC, a group called the Small Tool People lived around the coasts of Alaska. These people carved beautiful tools and weapons from bones and teeth. They made spears to hunt game and needles to sew animal skins into warm clothing. By 1000BC, another group called the Dorset People had come to dominate Arctic North America. They roamed the coastal waters in sea canoes, hunting seals and walruses. Two thousand years later, a third group, the Thule People, took over from the Dorsets. The Thule lived in houses built of turf and stone, used sledges pulled by dogs to travel over the ice and hunted huge bowhead whales.

The first Europeans to contact the Arctic peoples were the Vikings in AD983. From the late 1500s, Europeans came to the Arctic in increasing numbers. Until about 1800, life in the Arctic had changed very little for thousands of years. After that time, it began to alter much more quickly.

Extent of summer

Nenet camp

Saami with Reindeer

EUROPE

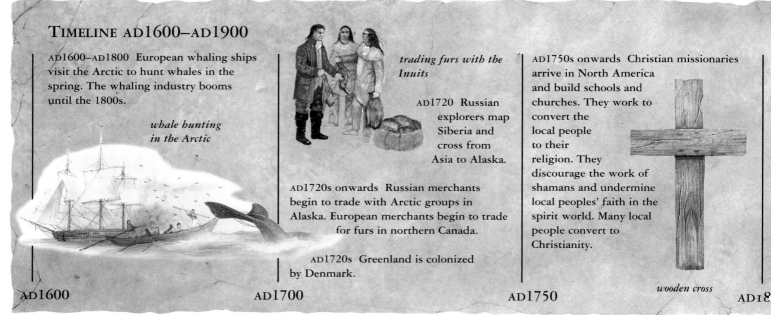

TIMELINE AD1600–AD1900

AD1600–AD1800 European whaling ships visit the Arctic to hunt whales in the spring. The whaling industry booms until the 1800s.

whale hunting in the Arctic

trading furs with the Inuits

AD1720 Russian explorers map Siberia and cross from Asia to Alaska.

AD1720s onwards Russian merchants begin to trade with Arctic groups in Alaska. European merchants begin to trade for furs in northern Canada.

AD1720s Greenland is colonized by Denmark.

AD1750s onwards Christian missionaries arrive in North America and build schools and churches. They work to convert the local people to their religion. They discourage the work of shamans and undermine local peoples' faith in the spirit world. Many local people convert to Christianity.

wooden cross

AD1600   AD1700   AD1750   AD18

FROZEN WORLD

This map shows the ancient Arctic world and also includes some of the main groups of people who still inhabit the Arctic region. The Arctic is shown during the summer.

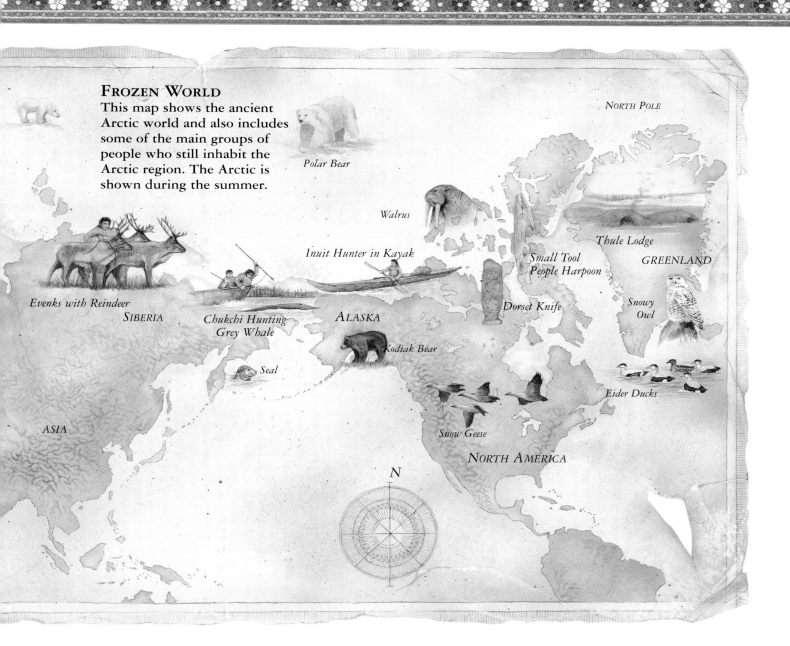

NORTH POLE

Polar Bear

Walrus

Inuit Hunter in Kayak

Thule Lodge

Small Tool People Harpoon

GREENLAND

Evenks with Reindeer

SIBERIA

Chukchi Hunting Grey Whale

ALASKA

Dorset Knife

Snowy Owl

Seal

Kodiak Bear

Eider Ducks

ASIA

Snow Geese

NORTH AMERICA

N

Hudson Bay trading certificate

AD1820 The Hudson Bay Trading Company, a British business, is set up in the Canadian Arctic. It soon controls the fur trade and a vast area of northern Canada. Native people trade skins for European items, such as rifles.

AD1867 Russia sells Alaska to the United States.

AD1870s Whaling declines in the Arctic, due to overhunting by European whalers.

AD1880–AD1890s A gold rush starts at the Yukon River and Klondike in Alaska. Many new settlers also move to the American Arctic. Gold is discovered in Siberia, and soon coal is mined there as well.

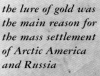

Alaska becomes part of the United States

AD1900s onwards European missionaries convert increasing numbers of Arctic peoples to Christianity. As the influence of southern nations increases, life in the Arctic changes more quickly. The people of Arctic America, Europe and Asia are made subject to their nations' laws.

the lure of gold was the main reason for the mass settlement of Arctic America and Russia

AD1850

AD1900

Peoples of the North

THE ARCTIC IS HOME to many different groups of people. These groups are the descendants of ancient races who have lived in these frozen lands for thousands of years. Each group has its own distinctive way of life, culture and language.

The Inuit are the most northerly group in the Arctic, living on the coasts of North America from Alaska through Canada to Greenland, and on the tip of eastern Asia. Many Inuit still follow the traditions of their ancestors, harpooning seals, walruses and other sea creatures. The peoples of Arctic Europe and Asia live farther south. The Saami, also called the Lapps, come from Scandinavia. Many Saami continue to herd reindeer for food. Northern Russia is home to more than 20 Arctic peoples. Groups such as the Chukchi, Evenks, Nenets and Yakut herd reindeer and also hunt game, just as their ancestors did before them.

CHUKCHI
A Chukchi man rests on one ski, which is covered in moose hide. The Chukchi came from northeastern Siberia, the part of Russia closest to North America. Traditionally, they have closer links with the Inuit than with any other group from Arctic Asia.

SAAMI
A Saami, or Lapp, man from Norway cuddles his son. The Saami were well-known for their colourful, traditional clothing, decorated with bright bands of red, yellow and blue woven ribbon. The Saami still live in Scandinavia but many have adopted a modern lifestyle.

TIMELINE AD1900–AD2000

AD1909 US explorer Robert Peary is the first to reach the North Pole, with the help of Inuit teams.

AD1917 After the Russian Revolution, the Soviets take power in Russia. The communist system is imposed in Siberia and throughout the new Soviet Union.

Robert Peary at the North Pole

a radar station in the middle of the Arctic

AD1939-1945 During World War II, army bases are set up throughout the Arctic.

AD1945-1980s As World War II ends, the Cold War begins between the Soviet Union and the West. Radar stations are set up across the Arctic to warn of missile attack. Gradually new communities grow up around these bases.

AD1968 Rich fields of oil and gas are discovered at Prudhoe Bay in Alaska. Mining increases in the Arctic, leading to pollution and the loss of some traditional hunting and herding grounds.

oil power station

AD1900   AD1930   AD1960   AD19[·]

EVENK

An Evenk man and woman show off their tame reindeer. These are draft animals, which means they are used for pulling sledges. In the frozen lands of northern Siberia in Russia, Evenks depend on reindeer for meat and for their hides, which are used to make warm clothing.

INUIT

This modern Inuit hunter's breath has frozen onto his beard. The Inuit used to be called Eskimos. This American Indian word means "eater of raw meat". However, most Inuit use the term *Inuit,* which means "the people". One Inuit man is called an Inuk.

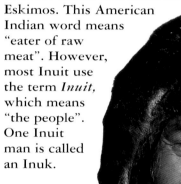

NENET

This Nenet girl is dressed in a warm coat made from reindeer skins. Nenets live over wide areas of Russia. Traditionally, these people live as nomads, travelling with the reindeer herds as they moved across the frozen Arctic wastes.

AD1977 Inuit and other Arctic peoples hold the first Inuit Circumpolar Conference. Arctic groups begin to organize, claiming traditional lands and demanding a say in their own affairs.

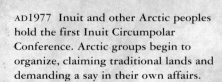

AD1979 Greenland wins home rule from Denmark.

the national flag of Greenland

seabird killed by an oil spill

AD1986 A fire at the nuclear power plant at Chernobyl in the Ukraine spreads radiation across the Arctic, polluting the reindeer pastures of the Saami and other Arctic herders.

AD1989 The wreck of the oil tanker *Exxon Valdez* pollutes the coast of Alaska and kills thousands of seabirds, otters and other creatures.

AD1990 Nunavut, a large territory in northern Canada, is awarded to the Inuit.

AD1999 The homeland of Nunavut is finally handed over to the Inuit.

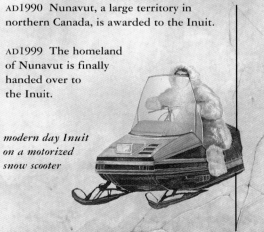

modern day Inuit on a motorized snow scooter

AD1980   AD1990   AD2000

A Frozen Land

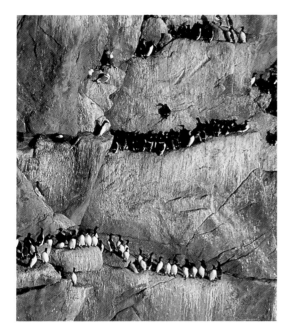

SUMMER VISITORS
In spring, birds, such as these guillemots, migrate to the Arctic in huge numbers. The guillemots nest on crowded cliff edges, to lay eggs and raise their young. Other birds nest in open tundra. As the harsh winter weather sets in, the birds move south again. Many Arctic peoples hunted summer visitors such as these.

THE ARCTIC is one of the coldest places on our planet. Freezing winter weather lasts for eight or nine months of the year. Summers provide a brief break from these harsh conditions. The polar regions – the Arctic in the north and the Antarctic in the far south – are so cold because the Sun never shines directly over them. Instead, it hangs low in the sky. The ice and snow also help to keep the temperature low because they reflect sunlight back into space.

Most of the Arctic region is actually an ocean, topped by drifting sheets of ice. In winter, most of the ocean surface freezes over. Temperatures on land are almost always colder than in the water. Greenland, the landmass nearest to the North Pole, is covered by a thick ice cap all year round. Further south, the areas of Asia, Europe and North America that lie within the Arctic Circle are mainly tundra – vast areas of barren, treeless lowlands. South of the tundra, a belt of dense, evergreen forests called the taiga dominates.

ICY LANDSCAPE
The Inuit village of Moriussaq in northern Greenland is covered by ice and snow for much of the year. In summer, temperatures rarely rise above 10°C. In winter, they often drop to −40°C. Throughout the Arctic region, the winter cold is so intense that the ground remains permanently frozen. This permanently frozen ground is known as permafrost. It may reach as deep as 600 metres in northernmost areas of the Arctic, such as Greenland and Siberia.

USEFUL PLANTS

Arctic peoples used the plants found in the region in many different ways. Some were eaten. For example, the leaves of the Arctic sorrel and the bark of the Arctic willow are rich in vitamins. Purple saxifrage yields a sweet nectar.

Purple saxifrage

Arctic willow

Arctic sorrel

WATERLOGGED SOIL

In the short Arctic summer, lakes, ponds and streams litter the surface of the Siberian tundra. In winter, the ground is permanently frozen. As summer approaches, however, the top layer of soil thaws. Water cannot penetrate the frozen layer below, so pools of water collect at the surface.

SPRING BLOOMS

In spring, Arctic plants, such as this yellow marsh saxifrage, quickly blossom. Flowering plants are found even in the far north of the Arctic. Many have special features that help them to cope with the bitterly cold conditions.

MIDNIGHT SUN

The midnight Sun lights up the pack ice covering the Arctic Ocean. The Sun never sets in the high Arctic during summer. In winter, it never rises, and the Arctic is a dark place. This is because the Earth tilts at an angle as it revolves around the Sun. In summer, the Arctic region leans towards the Sun, but in winter it tilts away.

NORTHERN LIGHTS

The northern lights or aurora borealis fill the skies over the Northwest Territories of Canada. The northern lights are an amazing display of red, yellow and green lights often seen in Arctic regions. They are caused by particles from the Sun striking Earth's atmosphere at the North Pole, releasing energy in the form of light.

Travelling with Reindeer

Some arctic peoples have long depended on the reindeer. This large mammal is found throughout the frozen Arctic region. In North America, where reindeer are known as caribou, wild herds roam the land in search of food. In Europe and Siberia, they have been domesticated (tamed) for hundreds of years. In ancient times, the Saami, Nenets, Chukchi and other Arctic groups depended on the reindeer as a source of food. These people used reindeer skins to make tents and warm clothes. They also shaped the bones and antlers into tools and weapons.

Many Arctic animals are migratory creatures, which means they travel in time with the changing seasons. Reindeer are no exception. In spring, huge herds move north towards the shores of the Arctic Ocean. They spend the summer grazing the tundra pastures. In autumn, they journey south again to spend the winter in the sheltered forests of the taiga. In the past, the Saami and Nenets travelled with the reindeer, moving the beasts on so they did not graze the pastures bare. Some of their descendants still live the same nomadic life.

TENDING YOUNG DEER
A Saami herdsman lifts a newborn calf. Reindeer calves are born in May and June, following the herd's migration to northern tundra pastures in the spring. Just a few hours after birth, most newborn calves are strong enough to stand up and walk.

REINDEER FOOD
Reindeer moss carpets the forest floor in Labrador, Canada. Reindeer moss is the main source of food for reindeer, since it is found beneath the snow in winter. In summer, a wider variety of plants is available for the reindeer to eat.

ROPING REINDEER
A Saami herder uses a modern rope lasso to catch a reindeer from the herd. In the past, Saami herdspeople used reindeer hide to make their lassos. Saami families owned herds of between 200 and 1000 animals. The size of the herd was an indication of the family's wealth.

ARCTIC ADAPTATIONS

A Chukchi herdsman checks his reindeer during a light snowstorm. Reindeer are well adapted to life in the harsh environment of the Arctic. They are warm-blooded mammals, and they must keep their bodies at a constant temperature to survive. A thick layer of insulating fur helps to keep each animal warm. Reindeer also have "heat exchangers" in their muzzles to warm the air they breathe in. Reindeer have broad hooves that help prevent the animals from sinking into the deep snow and becoming stranded.

FENCED IN

A Saami herder uses a long, billowing cloth to drive his animals into a fenced corral. Reindeer herds were driven into corrals to check their health and to decide which animals were the best to kill. The herder also saw if he had another herder's reindeer.

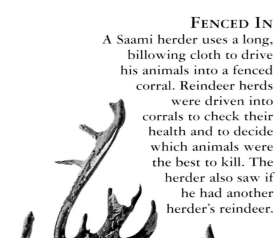

VALUED ANIMAL

Reindeer were extremely useful animals. They provided meat, and their blood and milk were drunk. Reindeer hides were used to make clothes, bedding and rough shelters. Bones and antlers were shaped into harpoons, needles and other tools and weapons. Even the animal's sinews (tendons) were used as sewing thread.

PACK LEADER

Traditionally, reindeer herds were led by tame deer wearing bells. Many Arctic Siberians kept male and female animals in separate groups.

milk

antler

hide

Settlements and Homes

MOST ANCIENT ARCTIC GROUPS lived in small villages containing a few families at most. The villages were spread out over a wide area, so each group had a large territory in which to hunt. In winter, the Inuit, Saami and other groups lived in sturdy houses built partly underground to protect them from the freezing conditions above. In summer, or when travelling from place to place, they lived in tents or temporary shelters.

In Siberia and parts of Scandinavia, groups such as the Nenets did not settle in one place. Their homes were lightweight tents, called chums in Siberia, made up of a framework of wooden poles and covered with animal skins. These chums could withstand severe Arctic blizzards and kept everyone warm inside when temperatures were icy.

TENT LIFE

A Nenet herder loads up a sledge outside his family's chum in preparation for another day's travel across Siberia. Chums were convenient, light and easy to assemble and dismantle. Some Nenets still live in chums, as their ancestors have done for generations.

BUILDING MATERIALS

A deserted building made from stone and whale bone stands on a cliff in Siberia. Building materials were scarce in the Arctic. In coastal regions, people built houses with whale bones and driftwood gathered from the beach. Inland, houses were mainly built with rocks and turf.

ARCTIC DWELLING

This illustration shows a house in the Alaskan subarctic with a portion cut away to show how it is made. Houses such as this one were buried under the ground. People entered by ladder through the roof.

MAKE A NENET TENT

You will need: 3 blankets (two at 2 x 1.5 m and one at 1.2 x 1.2 m), tape measure, string, scissors, 10 bamboo sticks (nine 180 cm long and one 30 cm long), black marker, black thread, a log or stone.

1 Cut small holes 10 cm apart along the shorter sides of the two large blankets. Thread a piece of string through the holes and tie the string together.

2 Cut a 60-cm length of string. Tie the 30-cm-long stick and a black marker 55 cm apart. Use the marker to draw a circle on the smaller blanket.

3 Tie four bamboo sticks together at one end. Open out the sticks onto the base blanket. Place the sticks on the edge of the circle so they stand up.

BONY BUNKER

Whale bone rafters arch over the remains of a home in Siberia. Part of the house was often built underground. First, the builders dug a pit to make the floor. Then they built low walls of rocks and turf. Long bones or driftwood laid on top of the walls formed sturdy rafters that supported a roof made from turf and stones.

MAKING WINDOWS

An old stone and turf house stands in Arctic Greenland. Ancient peoples made windows by stretching a dried seal bladder over a hole in the wall. The bladder was thin enough to allow light through.

A tent covered with several layers of animal skins made an extremely warm Arctic home, even in the bitterly cold winter. The wooden poles were lashed together with rope.

4 Lean the five extra bamboo sticks against the main frame, placing the ends around the base circle. Leave a gap at the front for the entrance.

5 Tie the middle of the edge of the two larger blankets to the back of the frame, at the top. Make two tight knots to secure the blankets.

6 Bring each blanket round to the entrance. Tie them at the top with string. Roll the blankets down to the base so they lie flat on the frame.

7 Tie five one-metre lengths of thread along the front edge of the blanket. Pull these tight and tie to a log or stone to weigh down the base of the tent.

Seasonal Camps

CHEERFUL GLOW
An igloo near Thule in Greenland is lit up by the glow of a primus stove. The light inside reveals the spiralling shape of the blocks of ice used to make the igloo. Snow crystals in the walls scatter the light so the whole room is bathed in the glow. In the Inuit language, *iglu* was actually a word to describe any type of house. A shelter such as this one was called an *igluigaq*.

S UMMER is a busy time for Arctic animals and plants. The rising temperature melts the sea ice, and the oceans teem with tiny organisms called plankton. On land, the tundra bursts into flower. Insects hatch out and burrowing creatures, such as lemmings, leave their tunnels in search of food. Wild reindeer, whales and many types of birds migrate to the Arctic to feast on the plentiful supply of food.

The lives of Arctic peoples changed with the seasons too. In Canada, Alaska and Greenland, the Inuit left their winter villages and travelled to the summer hunting grounds. They hunted fish and sea mammals and gathered fruits and berries, taking advantage of the long, bright summer days.

During winter hunting trips, the Inuit built temporary shelters made of snow blocks, commonly called igloos. The basic igloo design was developed hundreds of years ago. It kept the hunters warm even in the harshest Arctic storm.

BUILDING AN IGLOO
An Inuk builds an igloo, using a long ice knife to cut large blocks of tightly packed snow. First, he lays a ring of ice blocks to make a circle up to 3 metres in diameter. Then, some of the blocks are cut to make them slope. As new blocks are added, the walls of the igloo begin to lean inwards, forming the familiar dome-shaped igloo. This method is exactly the same as the one used by his ancestors centuries ago.

MAKE A MODEL IGLOO

You will need: self-drying clay, rolling pin, cutting board, ruler, modelling tool, scissors, thick card (20 x 20 cm), pencil, water bowl, white paint, paint brush.

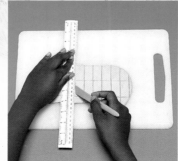

1 Roll out the self-drying clay. It should be around 8 mm thick. Cut out 30 blocks of clay; 24 must be 2 x 4 cm and the other 6 blocks must be 1 x 2 cm.

2 Cut out some card to make an irregular shape. Roll out more clay (8 mm thick). Put the template on the clay and cut around it to make the base of the igloo.

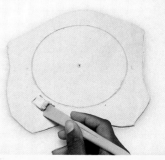

3 Mark out a circle with a diameter of 12 cm. Cut out a small rectangle on the edge of the circle (2 x 4 cm) to make the entrance to the igloo.

IGLOO VILLAGE

This engraving, made in 1871, shows a large Inuit village in the Canadian Arctic. Most Inuit igloos were simple, dome-like structures. The Inuit built these temporary shelters during the winter hunting trips.

THE FINAL BLOCK

An Inuit hunter carefully places the final block of ice onto the roof of his igloo. Ancient hunters used sharp ice knives to shape the blocks so that they fitted together exactly. Any gaps were sealed with snow to prevent the icy winds from entering the shelter.

A SNUG HOME

An Inuit hunter shelters inside his igloo. A small entrance tunnel prevents cold winds from entering the shelter and traps warm air inside. Outside, the temperature may be as low as −70°C. Inside, heat from the stove, candles and the warmth of the hunter's body keeps the air at around 5°C.

Inuit hunters built temporary shelters by fitting ice blocks together to form a spiralling dome structure called an igloo. Only firmly packed snow was used to make the building blocks.

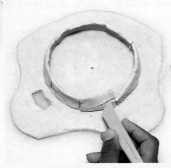

4 Stick nine large blocks around the edge of the circle. Use water to make the clay stick to the base. Cut across two rectangular blocks as shown above.

5 Using your modelling tool, carefully cut a small piece of clay from the corner of each of the remaining blocks as shown above.

6 Starting from the two blocks cut earlier, build up the walls, slanting each block in as you go. Use the six small blocks at the top. Leave a hole at the top.

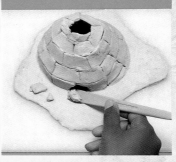

7 Use the modelling tool to form a small entrance to the igloo behind the rectangle already cut into the base. When the clay has dried, paint the igloo white.

Home Comforts

INSIDE ARCTIC SHELTERS, small comforts made life more bearable. From the earliest times, the Inuit and other Arctic groups used the frozen ground for sleeping platforms, or made them out of snow. Animal skins were draped across the platforms to make them warm and comfortable. Often, the walls and floor were lined with skins to provide extra insulation from the bitter Arctic winds.

The floor of the ancient Nenet and Saami tents was a meshwork of branches covered with animal skins. In the centre of the tent, flat stones made a safe platform for the fire. Arctic peoples started fires with the heat created by a tool called a bow drill. In Inuit shelters, stone lamps burning seal or whale fat provided heat and lit up the darkness. With lamps or candles burning, the shelters were surprisingly warm, and many people took off the outer layers of their clothing as they entered.

ROCKING THE CRADLE
A Nenet baby sleeps in its cradle. The cradle is usually suspended from the stout wooden struts that hold up the tent. The struts make a frame sturdy enough to support fairly heavy weights.

INSIDE AN IGLOO
This engraving of the inside of an igloo was made by the European traveller Edward Finden in 1824. Inuit women hung all their possessions from strings, poles and even reindeer antlers to warm them in the dry air higher in the igloo.

MAKE AN OIL LAMP
You will need: self-drying clay, rolling pin, cutting board, ruler, compass, sharp pencil, modelling tool, water bowl, dark grey and light grey paint, small paint brush.

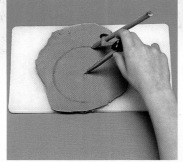

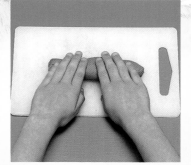

1 Roll out a piece of clay to a thickness of 1 cm. Draw out a circle with a radius of 5 cm, and carefully use the modelling tool to cut the circle out.

2 Using your hands, roll another piece of clay out into a long sausage shape. Make the shape around 30 cm long and 2 cm thick.

3 Wet the edge of the clay circle and stick the sausage shape around it. Use the rounded end of the modelling tool to blend the edges into the base.

FEEDING THE STOVE

A Nenet woman adds another log to the stove to keep her family's reindeer-skin tent warm. She has hung a pair of wet boots above the stove to dry them out. Stoves such as this one were light enough to be carried on sledges pulled by reindeer when it was time to move on.

IN THE FIRELIGHT

A Saami herder warms his hands in the light of a crackling fire inside his tent. You can see a large stack of wood piled up by the fire. Traditionally, the tent floor was a network of birch branches with skins laid over the top. Smoke spiralled upwards and escaped through a hole in the roof.

FIRE AND ICE

Two hunters sit on a skin-covered sleeping platform, keeping warm beside the fire. Most fires were balanced on frames made from driftwood or animal bones. That way, the flames did not go out or melt the floor. Wet clothes and animal skins were often dried on a rack set above the fire.

Stone lamps burning seal or whale blubber (fat) have long cast a warm glow in homes throughout the Arctic. A lighted wick of moss or fur was placed in a bowl filled with the fat and left to burn slowly.

4 Use your modelling tool to cut a small triangular notch at the edge of the circle. This will make a small lip for the front of the lamp.

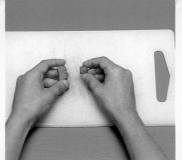

5 Shape a piece of clay into a small head. Use another piece to shape some shoulders. Stick the head to the shoulders by wetting the clay.

6 Stick the small figure just off the centre of the base of the lamp. Then use the modelling tool to make a small groove on the base to hold the oil.

7 Decorate the edge of the lamp with extra pieces of clay. Once dry, paint the lamp. *Safety note: do not attempt to burn anything in your model lamp.*

Family Life

ARCTIC PEOPLES lived in closely knit families. Most family groups were made up not just of a mother, father and their children, but often grandparents, uncles, aunts and cousins too. These family units often consisted of a dozen people or more, all living in extremely close quarters.

Within the family, men and women had different jobs to do. In Inuit society, men were responsible for hunting. They also maintained the hunting equipment and looked after the dogs that pulled their sledges. Women were responsible for most other chores around the home. Their work included tending the fire, cooking, fetching ice to make drinking water, preparing animal hides and looking after their children. Sewing was another important job for women. They had to find time to make and repair all the family's clothes and bedding. Surviving in the Arctic was hard, and both men and women often worked long hours to keep everyone warm, clothed and fed.

DIVIDING THE WORKLOAD
A Nenet woman pours tea for her husband inside the family tent. In Nenet families, work was divided among members of the family. Traditionally, men herded reindeer. Women did most other tasks. As well as cooking, women pitched and dismantled the tents, chopped wood, prepared animal hides and sewed all the family's clothing.

ALL-PURPOSE KNIFE
This knife, called an *ulu*, was the traditional tool of Inuit women. It was used for many tasks, including cutting meat and preparing animal hides. The *ulu* had a round blade, made from polished slate or metal. The handle was made from bone or wood.

DRAWSTRING PURSE
You will need: shammy leather (21 x 35 cm), PVA glue, glue brush, pencil, ruler, scissors, shoelace (50 cm long), red, dark blue and light blue felt, 2 blue beads.

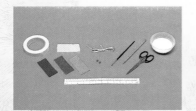

1 Fold over the piece of shammy leather to make a square shape. Glue down two opposite edges, leaving one end open. Let the glue dry.

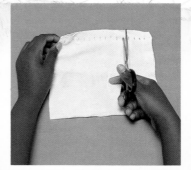

2 Across the open end of the purse, pencil in marks 1 cm apart on both sides of the leather. Use your scissors to make small holes at these points.

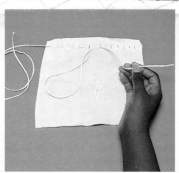

3 Thread a shoelace through the holes on both sides, as shown above. Tie the ends of the shoelace together and leave an excess piece of lace hanging.

CHOPPING ICE

Ice splinters fly as an Inuit hunter chops at a frozen block near a river in the Northwest Territories of Canada. Fetching ice to make drinking water was often a job for women. Once collected, the ice was taken back to the camp and melted over lamps that burned whale or seal blubber (fat).

USING FEATHERS

Arctic women often used the feathers of eider ducks, called eiderdown, to make bedding and warm clothes. Female ducks pluck these feathers from their breasts to help keep their chicks warm in the nest. Women collected the down from the nests or used bird skins complete with feathers. Eiderdown is still used today to make warm quilts.

Eider duck

DRYING SEALSKIN

An Inuit woman stretches a sealskin on a wooden frame to prevent the skin from shrinking as it dries. Preparing animal skins was a woman's job. Using her *ulu,* she would clean the skin by scraping off all the flesh and fat. Then the skin was stretched and dried. Finally, she would soften the hide by chewing it with her front teeth.

FEEDING TIME

An Inuit hunter feeds seal meat to each of his huskies. The Inuits used huskies as draft animals, and they were well looked after by their owners. In winter, they were fed extra meat to provide them with enough energy to pull a heavy sledge in the cold climate.

4 Carefully cut two strips of red felt 21 cm long and 5 cm wide. Then, cut a narrow fringe about 1 cm deep along both edges of the felt, as shown above.

5 Glue the strips of red felt to either side of the purse. You can add extra decoration by gluing 1 cm strips of blue felt on other parts of the purse.

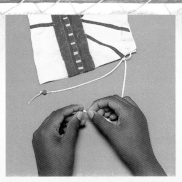

6 Tie the two blue beads firmly to each end of the excess shoelace. Close the purse by pulling the shoelace and tying a knot in it.

Arctic women often made bags, baskets and other useful containers. Drawstring purses such as this one were made of soft deer hide.

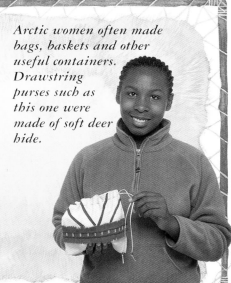

21

Arctic Children

MODEL IGLOO

An Inuit toddler plays with a model igloo at a nursery in the Canadian Arctic. The blocks of wood spiral upwards in the same way as the blocks of ice do in a real igloo, so the toy helps modern children to learn the ancient art of building igloos.

CHILDREN were at the centre of most Arctic societies. Inuit babies and younger children spent most of their time riding on their mother's back, nestled in a snug pouch called an *amaut*. The babies of many Arctic groups were named for a respected member of the community and their birth was celebrated with a huge feast. As children grew older, other members of the family helped the mother to bring up her child.

Today, most Arctic children go to school when they are young. However, the children of past generations travelled with their parents as the group moved to fresh reindeer pastures or new hunting grounds. Very young boys and girls were treated equally. As they grew up, however, children helped with different tasks and learned the skills that they would need later on in life. Boys learned how to hunt and look after animals. Girls learned to sew and cook and to work with animal skins.

BIRTHDAY FEAST

Traditional food is prepared at the birthday celebration of the young boy sitting at the table. Parents often named their newborn babies after people who had been respected in the community, such as a great hunter. The baby was thought to inherit that person's skills and personality.

FEEDING BIRDS TOY

You will need: self-drying clay, rolling pin, ruler, modelling tool, board, two toothpicks, white and brown paint, water pot, paint brush.

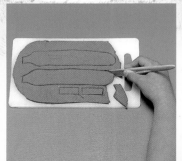

1 Roll out some of the clay into a 22 x 14 cm rectangle with a thickness of around 1 cm. Cut out two large paddles (18 x 3 cm) and two stalks (4 x 2 cm).

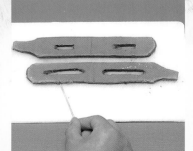

2 Cut two slots on paddle 1 (5 cm x 8 mm) and two on paddle 2 (2.5 cm x 8 mm). Use a toothpick to pierce a hole in the side of paddle 1 through these slots.

3 Roll out two egg shapes, each about 5 x 3.5 cm, in the palm of your hands. Make two bird heads and stick them to the egg-shaped bodies.

LENDING A HAND

A Nenet boy and his younger brother help to feed a reindeer calf that has lost its mother. Fathers taught their sons to handle animals from a very early age. Children were encouraged to look after the family's tame deer and dogs.

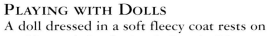

RIDING HIGH

One of the children in this old illustration is being carried in a special hood, called an *amaut*, high on the back of his mother's jacket. The second child is tucked inside her mother's sealskin boots. However, it was less common for a child to be carried in this way.

PLAYING WITH DOLLS

A doll dressed in a soft fleecy coat rests on a Nenet sledge in Arctic Russia. Many Arctic girls like to play with dolls, as children do around the world. Traditionally, the dolls' heads were carved from ivory. The doll in the picture, however, is made of modern plastic.

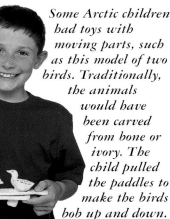

Some Arctic children had toys with moving parts, such as this model of two birds. Traditionally, the animals would have been carved from bone or ivory. The child pulled the paddles to make the birds bob up and down.

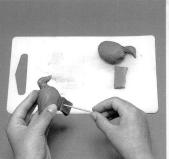

4 Stick the stalks you made earlier to the base of each bird's body. Using the toothpick, pierce a small hole through the stalk, close to the body.

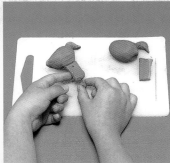

5 Leave the clay bird to dry on its side. You will need to support the stalk with a small piece of clay to hold the bird upright as it dries.

6 Place the stalk of each bird in the slots in the paddles. Push a toothpick into the holes in the edge of paddle 1, through the stalks and out the other side.

7 Add two small pieces of clay to the bottom of each stalk to keep the birds in place. You can paint the toy once the clay has dried.

23

Fun and Games

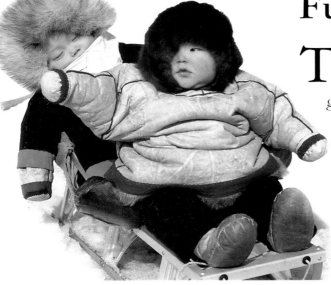

THE EARLY YEARS were exciting times for Arctic children, with plenty of time for play and fun. Outdoor games included sliding and sledging on the ice. Indoors, children played traditional games or learned to carve animal bones. In the evenings, everyone gathered round the fire, and adults would tell magical stories featuring brave warriors and terrible monsters. For example, the Saami of Scandinavia told their children tales about *Stallos* – scary monsters that liked to eat people. The hero of the story had to outwit the monster to avoid being eaten.

Ivory, bones, animal hides and sinew (tendons) were all used to make various games and toys. Balls were made from inflated seal bladders.

The tiny bones from a seal's flipper were used to make an Inuit version of the game of jacks.

SLEDGING IN THE SNOW
Two children enjoy a toboggan ride in Siberia. Boys and girls who live in the Arctic love to play in the snow. Sledging and playing in the snow help to teach children about the different snow conditions that exist in the region.

GOING HUNTING
An Inuit hunter teaches his son how to read tracks in the snow. Boys learned vital hunting skills from an early age. A boy's first kill was very important and a day he would remember for the rest of his life. To mark the occasion, the boy's parents might hold a feast for all the family to attend. Around the age of twelve, boys were allowed to go on more dangerous hunting trips with their fathers, such as walrus- or whale-hunting expeditions.

HOLE AND PIN GAME
You will need: thin card, ruler, pencil, PVA glue, glue brush, masking tape, scissors, compass, 40 cm length of black thread, thick card, cream paint, paint brush, water pot, chopstick.

1 Using the thin card, mark out a triangle with a base 13 cm long and a height of 15 cm. Roll the triangular piece of card around a pencil to soften it.

2 Shape the softened card into a cone and glue it into position. You may need to secure the cone with a piece of masking tape.

3 Once you have secured it into position, trim off the excess card from the base of the cone. Make sure you always cut away from your body.

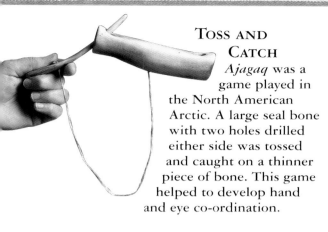

TOSS AND CATCH

Ajagaq was a game played in the North American Arctic. A large seal bone with two holes drilled either side was tossed and caught on a thinner piece of bone. This game helped to develop hand and eye co-ordination.

LASSOING GAME

A Chukchi boy from Arctic Russia learns to use a lasso by practising on a reindeer antler. This skill will be essential later on in life. Around the Arctic, various games were played with reindeer antlers. Sometimes children would run around with the antlers on their heads, pretending to be reindeer. The other children would try to lasso or herd them.

STRING PUZZLES

An Inuit woman from Greenland shows a traditional puzzle she has made by winding string around her fingers. The shape depicts two musk oxen – large, fearsome Arctic mammals – charging each other. String puzzles were a common way of passing the time during the long Arctic winter. The strings were made from whale sinew (tendons) or long strips of sealskin.

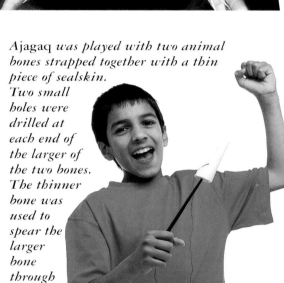

Ajagaq was played with two animal bones strapped together with a thin piece of sealskin. Two small holes were drilled at each end of the larger of the two bones. The thinner bone was used to spear the larger bone through one of the holes.

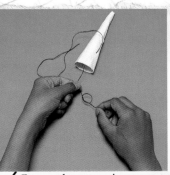

4 Cover the cone in tape. Pierce a hole in the middle of the cone, thread some black thread through, tie a knot on the inside and secure it with tape.

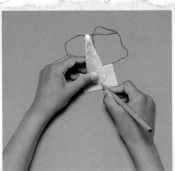

5 Use the base of the cone to draw a circle onto the thicker piece of card. Carefully cut around the circle using your pair of scissors.

6 Pierce lots of holes through the thick card circle, making sure the chopstick will fit through them. Glue this piece onto the base of the cone.

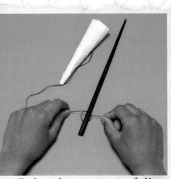

7 Paint the cone carefully, avoiding the holes. Once it has dried, secure the chopstick to the other end of the thread using a tight knot, as shown above.

Over Ice and Snow

DURING THE WINTER, the surface of the Arctic Ocean freezes over and snow covers the land. In the past, sledges were the most common way of travelling over the ice and snow. They were made from bone or timber lashed together with strips of hide or whale sinew. They glided over the snow on runners made from walrus tusks or wood. Arctic sledges had to be light enough to be pulled by animals, yet strong enough to carry an entire family and its belongings. In North America, the Inuit used huskies to pull their sledges. In Siberia and Scandinavia, however, reindeer were used to pull sledges.

In ancient times, Arctic peoples sometimes used skis and snowshoes to get around. Skis are thought to have been invented by the Saami more than 3,500 years ago. Snowshoes allowed Arctic hunters to stalk prey without sinking into deep snowdrifts.

REINDEER SLEDGES
Three reindeer stand by a family and their sledge in Siberia. In Arctic Russia and Scandinavia, reindeer were commonly used to pull sledges. Small, narrow sledges carried just one person. Larger, wider models could take much heavier loads.

HITCHING A DOG TEAM
A husky team struggles up a hill in eastern Greenland. Traditionally, the reins, or traces, used by the dogs to pull the sledge, were made of walrus hide. Different cultures used one of two arrangements to hitch the dogs together. Some people hitched them in the shape of a fan. Others hitched the dogs as pairs in a long line.

MODEL SLEDGE

You will need: thick card, balsa wood, ruler, pencil, scissors, PVA glue, glue brush, masking tape, compass, barbecue stick, string, shammy leather, brown paint, paint brush, water pot.

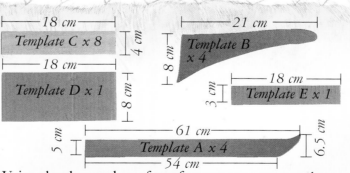

— 18 cm —
Template C x 8   4 cm
— 18 cm —   8 cm
Template D x 1

— 21 cm —
Template B x 4   8 cm

— 18 cm —
3 cm Template E x 1

5 cm — 61 cm —   6.5 cm
Template A x 4
— 54 cm —

Using the shapes above for reference, measure out the shapes on the card (use balsa wood for template C). Cut the shapes out using your scissors. You will need to make 4 A templates, 4 B templates, 8 C templates (balsa wood), 1 D template and 1 E template. Always remember to cut away from your body when using scissors.

1 Glue 2 A templates together. Repeat this for the other 2 A templates. Repeat this with the 4 B templates. Cover all the edges with masking tape.

SNOWSHOES

Snowshoes are used to walk across deep snowdrifts without sinking into the snow. They spread the person's weight across a large area. To make the snowshoe, thin, flexible birch saplings were steamed to make them supple. The saplings were then bent into the shape of the snowshoe frame. Some shoes were rounded but others were long and narrow. The netting was woven from long strips of animal hide.

birch sapling

rawhide thongs

snowshoes

MAN'S BEST FRIEND

This picture, painted around 1890, shows an Inuit hunter harnessing one of his huskies. Huskies were vital to Inuit society. Out on the hunt, the dogs helped to nose out seals hiding in their dens and hauled heavy loads of meat back to camp.

SAAMI SKIS

The Saami have used skis for thousands of years. The skis were made of wood and the undersides were covered with strips of reindeer skin. The hairs on the skin pointed backwards, allowing the skier to climb up hills.

LET SLEEPING DOGS LIE

A husky's thick coat keeps it warm in temperatures as low as −50°C. These hardy animals can sleep peacefully in the fiercest of blizzards. The snow builds up against their fur and insulates them.

Inuit hunters used wooden sledges pulled by huskies to hunt for food over a large area. The wood was lashed together with animal hide or sinew.

2 Using a compass, make small holes along the top edge of the glued A templates. Use the end of a barbecue stick to make the holes a little larger.

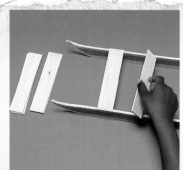

3 Glue the balsa wood slats C in position over the holes along the A templates as shown above. You will need to use all 8 balsa wood slats.

4 Carefully glue the B templates and the E and D templates to the end of the sledge, as shown above. Allow to dry, then paint the model.

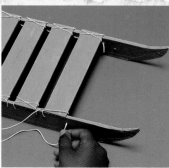

5 Thread string through the holes to secure the slats on each side. Decorate the sledge with a shammy-covered card box and secure it to the sledge.

On the Water

IN THE SUMMER, as soon as the sea ice had melted, Arctic people took to the water to hunt. Inuit hunters used one-person canoes called *kayaks* to track their prey. *Kayaks* were powered and steered by a double-bladed paddle. To make the craft more waterproof, the hunter closed up the top of his *kayak*. leaving only a narrow gap to allow him to climb in. The design was so successful that *kayaks* are still in use today.

Kayaks were light, speedy craft, ideal for the solitary hunter to chase seals and small whales. When hunting large bowhead whales, however, Inuit men teamed up into hunting parties of up to ten people and travelled in bigger, open boats called *umiaks*. These craft were also used to transport families across stretches of water and to ferry heavy loads from place to place.

KAYAK TRIP

An engraving made in the 1860s shows an Inuit hunter in a *kayak* chasing a small Arctic whale called a narwhal. The hunter's harpoon is attached to a large float, which is designed to slow down the harpooned whale and prevent its body from sinking when it dies. The hunter's equipment is securely lashed to the *kayak* using thick straps of animal hide.

BUILDING A KAYAK

An Inuit craftsman shapes the final pieces of his *kayak* frame. Traditionally, the wooden frame was covered with sealskins that were sewn together with skillful waterproof seams. All the joints were shaped to fit together exactly or secured with wooden pegs or leather strips.

MODEL UMIAK

You will need: shammy leather, thick card, thin card, 5 mm dowel, ruler, pencil, scissors, PVA glue, glue brush, masking tape, brown paint, paint brush, water pot, needle, brown thread.

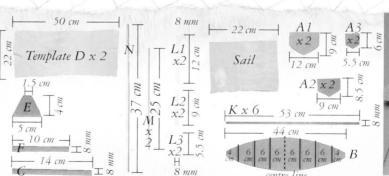

1 Use shammy leather to make the sail and template D. Cut 2 thick card templates A1, A2 and A3. Cut 6 thick card templates K. Use thick card to cut template B. Cut 10 thick card templates C, 4 templates F and 2 templates E. Using the dowel, cut template N and 2 templates M. Templates L1, L2 and L3 should be cut from thin card.

2 Mark the centre, then mark cutting lines at 6 cm, 12 cm and 18 cm either side of the centre of template B. Use the scissors to cut along the lines.

UPTURNED *UMIAK*

A photograph taken in Alaska around 1900 shows an Inuit family sheltering inside an upturned *umiak*. *Umiaks* were made of seal or walrus skins stretched over a sturdy wooden or bone frame. They were used to transport large hunting parties or heavy loads.

TREACHEROUS WATERS

A large iceberg drifts in the sea off the coast of Greenland. Arctic waters held many dangers for Inuit hunters. Icebergs were a particular problem when they broke up or rolled. In summer, melting ice at the water's edge made it difficult to get in and out of boats. If a hunter slipped and fell into the icy water, he would last only minutes before dying of exposure.

KAYAK PADDLE

An Inuit hunter shapes a new paddle from a wooden plank. Traditional *kayak* paddles were double-bladed, which made it easier to keep the boat steady in rough seas. The twin blades also allowed the hunters to move through the water more quickly as they pursued their prey.

TRAVEL BY *UMIAK*

Three Inuit hunters paddle a small *umiak* though the icy waters off the coast of Alaska. *Umiaks* were more stable than *kayaks* in rough seas and when hunting larger sea mammals. However, they were much heavier to haul over the ice to the water's edge.

3 Glue the middle section of A onto the sections of template B, as shown above. Use the smallest A templates at the end. Use the largest A template at the centre.

4 Glue 2 strips of template K to both sides of the structure, as shown above. Glue the K templates together at each end of the structure.

5 Weave templates C through templates K and over templates A, as shown. Fix with glue. Leave 1.5 cm excess card at the top of the boat.

6 Stick the ends of C together with masking tape. Repeat the last two stages with F for the smaller ends of the structure.
Continued on next page...

Tools and Weapons

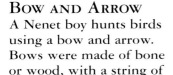

ARCTIC HUNTERS used many different weapons, hand-crafted from materials such as animal hide, bone and ivory. Weapons were kept in the best possible condition, and the hunter would inspect his weapons carefully before setting off each day.

Traditional Arctic weapons included bows and arrows and slingshots, used to bring down game birds, reindeer and other prey. Long three-pronged spears, called *kakivaks,* were used to catch fish. Seals, whales and other sea creatures were hunted with harpoons. Many weapons had barbed tips that lodged in the wounded animal's flesh. Other hunting tools included nets, fish hooks and sun goggles. When hunting in *kayaks,* western Inuits of Alaska or Asia, called Yupiks, wore wooden helmets to protect their eyes from the glare of the sun.

BOW AND ARROW
A Nenet boy hunts birds using a bow and arrow. Bows were made of bone or wood, with a string of twisted sinew. The arrow tips were made from ivory or copper.

SNOW GOGGLES
These Inuit snow goggles are made from the antlers of a reindeer. The hunter peered through the narrow slits. Snow goggles protected hunters' eyes from the reflection of the Sun on the snow, which could cause temporary "snow blindness".

FISH SPEAR
An Inuit hunter holds a traditional three-pronged spear called a *kakivak* during a fishing trip in northern Canada. The triple prongs of the spear lodge securely in the flesh of the fish so that it cannot wriggle free and swim away.

7 Glue the remaining K templates to the sides and ends of the structure as before. Pierce a hole for the mast in the middle of the base of the boat.

8 Glue in templates E to both ends of the structure, as shown above. Now paint the inside of the boat and leave it to dry.

9 Cover the sides of the boat with the shammy leather templates D. Stretch and glue the leather into position, as shown above. Leave the base hanging free.

10 Cut two small slits in the base of templates D. Overlap and curve the leather templates around the base of the structure, as shown above.

HARPOON AT THE READY
A harpoon rests in the prow of a boat off the coast of Alaska. The harpoon is attached to a float with a length of rope. This makes sure the weapon will not sink and can be retrieved if the hunter misses his target.

BIRD NET
An Arctic hunter checks his net, called a *lpu*, for damage. In summer, these nets were used to catch birds known as little auks.

HARPOON MAKING
Harpoons were versatile weapons, used to hunt seals, whales and walruses. Each weapon was carefully crafted. Wood and ivory were fitted together to form the shaft and the ivory point was tipped with metal such as copper. The head detached from the shaft on impact. It was securely fastened to a long hide line, in turn the line was attached to a float made of wood or an inflated seal bladder. Today, hunters use a nylon line attached to a float made from an inner tube.

copper

harpoon head

HANDY PICK
This Inuit pick is made of a walrus tusk bound to a wooden handle with thin strips of animal hide. Picks such as this one would have been used to hack away at frozen soil or to smash through thick blocks of ice.

Umiaks were large open boats that were around 9 metres (30 feet) long. They carried up to ten people and were powered by oars or a sail. Umiaks were used for transport or for hunting. Women sometimes helped to row the boats.

11 Glue the base of templates D into position, as shown above. Stretch the ends of the shammy leather tight to make a neat join.

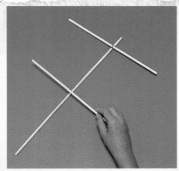

12 Glue the balsa mast templates M 2 cm and 17 cm down from the top of template N, as shown above. Secure all the pieces with thread.

13 Paint the mast and leave it to dry. Then, carefully stitch the sail to the mast using large overhead stitches, as shown above.

14 Glue and tape the sail into position using the hole you made before. Glue templates L over section pieces A to make seats, and then paint them.

Going Hunting

ARCTIC PEOPLE were skilled hunters. For most of the year, their diet consisted only of meat. In Russia and Scandinavia, the Saami and other herding peoples ate reindeer meat. In North America and Greenland, the Inuit's main source of food was seals. (In fact, the Inuit word for seal means "giver of life".) Many land animals, such as Arctic hares, musk oxen and nesting birds, were also eaten. Out on the ice or in the water, hunters chased polar bears, fish, walruses and whales.

Only the men went hunting. During the summer, hunters in boats stalked seals and walruses in the water. When the sea froze over in winter, the same creatures were hunted on foot. Arctic hunters worked all year round to provide their families with enough food, even during the long, dark winter days when the Sun never rose in the sky.

GOOD FISHING
An Inuk from eastern Greenland sits on his sledge, fishing for halibut through a hole in the ice. He has already caught four fish. Arctic hunters used hooks, nets and spears to catch their prey. In summer, fish were usually taken from lakes or from their river spawning grounds.

STALKING SEALS
A drawing from the 1820s shows two Inuit waiting at seals' breathing holes. In summer, seals climb up onto the ice to sleep in the sunlight. Inuit hunters stalked these seals on foot. If the seal awoke, the hunter would lie on the ice, pretending to be another seal. The best hunters could crawl right up to a seal, grab it by the flipper and club it to death.

HUNTING BLIND

You will need: dark green felt (90 x 65 cm), scissors, ruler, string, 6 bamboo sticks (two 80 cm long and four 55 cm long), masking tape, PVA glue, glue brush, light green felt, pencil, leaves.

1 Fold the dark green felt in half along its length. Using your scissors, cut a small hole in the centre of the felt on the fold, as shown above.

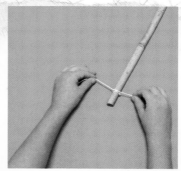

2 Tie a length of string to one end of two 55 cm lengths of bamboo. Use tape to hold the string in position, leaving a 10 cm length of string hanging.

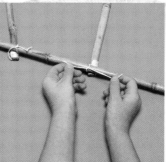

3 Tie the ends of these two 55 cm long bamboo poles to the area around the middle of one of the 80 cm lengths of bamboo, as shown above.

UNDER COVER

Today, modern Inuit hunters use rifles for hunting prey. The Inuk pictured above is also using a screen called a hunting blind to stalk a seal. The hunting blind conceals the hunter from the watchful eyes of seals. Both the screen and rifle are mounted on a small sledge, which allows the hunter to advance slowly towards his target.

IN FOR THE KILL

This engraving shows an Inuit hunter aiming his harpoon at a seal that has come to the surface of the water to breathe. Silent and motionless, hunters would wait at these breathing holes for hours if necessary. The tiniest noise or vibration at the surface would frighten the animal away. When the seal finally surfaced, the hunter would spear it and drag it from the hole. The hunter would then kill the seal by clubbing it over the head.

NETTING BIRDS

An Inuk nets a little auk on the rocky slopes of Pitufik in northwest Greenland. In spring, millions of birds migrate to the Arctic to lay eggs and rear their young. The Inuit and other groups caught these birds by using nets or by throwing weighted strings, known as *bolas,* at the birds.

The Inuit and other Arctic peoples used hunting blinds to sneak up on prey, such as seals. Most hunting blinds were white so they blended in with the snow. A green blind would work better in a leafy landscape.

4 Glue the other 55 cm bamboo poles to the two shorter edges of the felt. Glue the last 80 cm pole to one of the longer edges. Tape the bamboo at the corners.

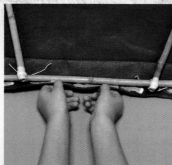

5 Glue the 80 cm bamboo pole from stage three to the fourth edge of the felt. Make sure to glue around the lengths of bamboo that are tied on.

6 Draw some leaf shapes on the light green felt, and use your scissors to cut the shapes out. Always cut away from your body when using scissors.

7 Decorate the hunting blind by sticking the leaves to the front of the screen. You can glue some real leaves to the hunting blind for more effect.

Big Game Hunters

As well as smaller prey, such as seals and fish, Arctic people also hunted large and dangerous creatures, such as musk oxen, whales and polar bears. Hunting these animals was a risky business. A huge whale could easily swamp and capsize an *umiak*. Stranded in the icy water, the hunters would die of exposure in a matter of minutes. A cornered polar bear was an equally dangerous creature. One swipe of its enormous paws was enough to kill any hunter. This fierce predator is also one of the few animals in the world that hunts humans.

Musk oxen were also well able to defend themselves. These large, hairy mammals had long, sharp horns that could impale an unfortunate hunter, inflicting a fatal wound. Hunting dangerous beasts such as these required a team of men and careful planning. If the hunters were successful, one kill could provide enough meat to feed their families for many days.

FEROCIOUS HUNTER

A polar bear stands over a seal it has caught in Arctic Norway. The polar bear is a fearsome creature, with its mighty claws and razor-sharp teeth. This did not deter Inuit hunters, however. They would set their dogs on a bear to keep it at bay, and spear it when they got close enough.

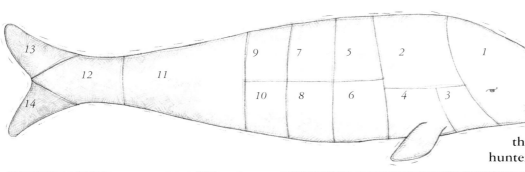

FAIR SHARES

When a white whale was killed, the animal was divided between the hunters so that everyone had a share of the meat. Whales were split up in a particular way. The man who threw the first harpoon got the whale's head and part of the underside (shares 1, 2, 3 and 10). Other hunters and the boat owner got other shares.

SNOW GOGGLES

You will need: a piece of thin card, ruler, pencil, scissors, shammy leather (22 x 6 cm), black pen, PVA glue, glue brush, compass, elastic.

20 cm
1 cm
4 cm

Eyeholes

6 cm
4 mm

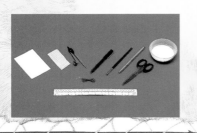

1 Cut the piece of card to 20 x 4 cm. Find the centre of the piece of card, and mark eyeholes 1 cm from the centre. The holes should be 6 cm x 4 mm.

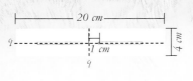

2 Carefully cut out the eyeholes using the ends of your scissors to pierce the card. Always cut away from your body when using scissors.

3 Place the card onto the piece of shammy leather. Use the card as a template and draw around the goggles shape. Remember to draw in the eyeholes.

A USEFUL CREATURE

Whales were valuable Arctic animals. Every part of a whale's body was used. The flesh, fat and internal organs were divided between all the hunters. Some of the meat was given to the dogs. The whale's skin, called *muktuk*, was eaten as a delicacy. The blubber was burned in lamps to provide light and heat. Finally, the huge bones were used to build shelters or carved into weapons and tools.

muktuk

whale bone

MUSK OX CIRCLE

A circle of musk oxen surround their young to protect them against predators. Musk oxen are peaceful tundra animals unless threatened. Then, the adults lower their heads and ward off attackers with their curving horns. Arctic hunters were wary of musk oxen but still hunted them for food.

WHALE HUNT

Teams of Inuit hunters used *umiaks* to hunt large whales, such as bowheads. The oarsmen kept the boat steady so that skilled marksmen could launch their harpoons at the whale. A wounded whale would attempt to dive or swim away, but floats attached to the harpoons would pull the whale back to the surface. Gradually, the animal would become exhausted. Finally, hunters lanced the animal to death and hauled it to the shore.

Arctic hunters used snow goggles when hunting both land and sea creatures. The narrow slits cut down the glare caused by sunlight reflecting on the snow and ice, so the hunter could see his prey more clearly.

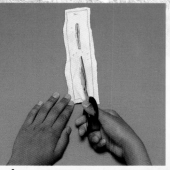

4 Cut round the goggles shape, leaving a small trim around the edge. Cut down the centre of the eyeholes you have drawn on the shammy leather.

5 Glue the card onto the shammy leather, making sure that you carefully match up the eyeholes on the leather and the card.

6 Fold back the leather trim and glue it to the back of the card. Open up the eyeholes, fold those edges back and glue them to the card.

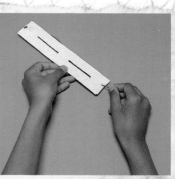

7 Pierce a small hole at either end of the goggles and thread elastic through the holes. Tie a knot at the end. Make sure the elastic fits around your head.

Hunting Magic

ARCTIC SOCIETIES had a great respect for nature and the animals they hunted. They believed that all creatures, like people, had spirits. When they killed an animal, they performed rituals that helped to appease (calm) the creature's spirit. The Inuit, for example, beheaded a slain beast to help the animal's spirit leave its body. They made offerings of food and drink in the hope that the animal's spirit would be reborn to be hunted again. Other Arctic hunters put parts of creatures they had killed back into the sea. Hunters took only what they needed to survive. They wasted nothing.

Arctic groups had many taboos, which were rules linked with spiritual practices. Hunting, in particular, was surrounded by many taboos. If a hunter broke a taboo, his action would anger the spirits and he might never hunt successfully again. Shamans were respected members of the community who talked to spirits. They provided a link between ordinary Arctic people and these powerful spirits. Shamans conducted ceremonies to bring good luck to hunting parties.

SACRED PILLAR
Inuksuk, pictured above, are stone columns built by Inuit groups in ancient times. Some are very old. They are linked with hunting taboos and some have a religious meaning. The pillars were built to resemble a person with his or her arms outstretched. (The Inuit word *inuksuk* means "like a person".) They marked routes and channelled migrating reindeer into places where hunters could ambush and kill them.

A RESPECTED BEAST
This ivory carving of a polar bear comes from Greenland. Many taboos surrounded the hunting of these highly respected creatures. The Inuit held polar bears in high esteem because they were thought to look and act in the same way as humans, particularly when they reared up on their hind legs.

WHALE BOX
This wooden box is carved in the shape of a whale. It held the lance points used to harpoon whales. The Inuit and other Arctic groups believed that prey animals, such as whales, were more likely to accept being killed by weapons carved in their image. The lance points would also experience being inside a "whale" and would therefore be more likely to hit their target.

MAGIC SCRATCHER

This "Nunivak tusk" was made as a souvenir in the 1920s. When hunting seals, the Inuit sometimes made screeching noises by scraping ivory scratchers such as this one over the ice. The noise attracted seals to within striking distance of their harpoons. Scratchers were often carved into the shape of the seal's head. Arctic hunters thought this would bring them good luck in future hunting trips.

SPRING CEREMONY

The Chukchi people offer sea spirits food at the edge of the water. The Chukchi took to the seashore early in the spring. They offered food to appease the spirits of the sea. This ritual helped to ensure that the year's hunting would be successful. Elsewhere, when a mighty whale was killed, the hunters held a festival to thank the sea spirits for their generosity.

SYMPATHETIC MAGIC

Drag handles were tools that helped hunters haul animals over the ice after they had been killed. The one shown here is decorated with the heads of three polar bears. Hunters' weapons were often carved to resemble the animals they hunted. This was sympathetic magic, which would help to appease the animal's spirit and bring the hunter good luck in future hunting expeditions.

Food and Feasts

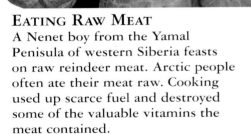

FOR MOST OF THE YEAR, Arctic people lived on a diet of fish and game known as "land food". The fat, flesh, organs and skin of seals, whales, reindeer and other animals contained all the proteins, minerals and vitamins needed for a healthy diet. Vegetables and grain crops, such as wheat, were difficult to grow in most parts of the Arctic region. Few plants could thrive in the frozen soil.

In winter, food was scarce and animals were the main source of food. In the summer, however, food was more varied. People feasted on berries, hunted seabirds and gathered eggs. Siberian and Saami women collected fungi that grew taller than Arctic plants, which were smaller. In autumn, when the reindeer were slaughtered, a great feast was held. Everyone kept very busy, gathering and storing food for the winter months ahead.

EATING RAW MEAT

A Nenet boy from the Yamal Penisula of western Siberia feasts on raw reindeer meat. Arctic people often ate their meat raw. Cooking used up scarce fuel and destroyed some of the valuable vitamins the meat contained.

DRYING MEAT

An Inuit hunter from northwest Greenland lays strips of narwhal meat on the rocks to dry them. Drying meat in this way was an excellent way of preserving food in the summer. The intestines were washed clean and also dried in this way. Meat was also hidden under the rocks to prevent foxes, wolverines and other carnivorous animals from stealing it. If the meat was left for many months, it developed a strong smell and flavour, but it was unlikely to make anyone ill. In winter, the icy temperatures prevented meat from going off, so preserving food was not a problem. The bodies of slain animals could be buried under rocks in the snow near the house and dug up when needed.

FILLETS OF FISH

Inuit hunters arrive back at the shore with a catch of fish known as char. Traditionally, women cleaned and filleted the fish, then hung them up on racks to dry and preserve them. They scored the fishes' flesh into squares to speed up the drying process.

BERRIES

Many types of berries grow wild on the Arctic tundra. They include bilberries, cranberries and cloudberries. Ripe berries contain valuable vitamins. Autumn was the time for picking berries, when they were eaten fresh, and could also be frozen.

bilberries   *cranberries*   *cloudberries*

BIRD'S EGGS

This picture shows three eggs in an eider duck's nest. In the spring, many nesting birds came to the Arctic to rear their young. Their eggs were a valuable source of food and protein for Arctic people and helped to vary the basic diet of meat.

SAAMI FARMERS

A Saami reindeer herder erects a tent by his summer pastures. In Scandinavia, the Saami are able to farm along the shores of narrow coastal inlets called fjords. On these jagged coasts the land is sheltered from icy winds, so cattle and sheep can graze. Some meadows are mown to make hay to feed the animals in winter.

TASTY MEAL

A Nenet woman cooks a meal for her family. In all Arctic societies it was the woman who did the cooking, making meat stews and other traditional dishes. Children often clustered around the fire to steal a taste from the pot.

The Coming of Europeans

BEFORE 1600, only a tiny handful of Europeans had ever visited the Arctic. After this time, however, travellers began to arrive in larger numbers. Explorers from Britain, France, Holland and Russia searched for a short cut to China and the Pacific Ocean through the seas north of Canada and Siberia. The sea route north of Canada was known as the Northwest Passage; the route north of Siberia was called the Northeast Passage. From the late 1500s, the British explored the northern coast of Canada. In the 1700s, the Russians mapped Siberia and travelled to Alaska, crossing a sea we now call the Bering Strait.

In the end, European explorers failed to find clear sea routes to the Pacific through the ice-laden waters of the Arctic Ocean. However, they did return with tales of waters teeming with whales and other sea creatures. Whaling ships and other hunters soon followed. Every spring, European ships would cross the northern Atlantic Ocean to slaughter whales. Arctic whale oil was used as a source of fuel for European lamps. These giant creatures were also killed for their valuable "whalebone", or baleen.

ARCTIC ATTACKERS
This early illustration shows a group of Inuit in conflict with English explorers led by a sea captain named Martin Frobisher. Frobisher led one of the first expeditions to Baffin Island in northeast Canada, where his sailors met with strong opposition from the local people.

VIKING RAIDERS
This early drawing shows Viking warriors attacking an Inuit settlement in Greenland. Vikings were the first Europeans to reach the Arctic. In AD983, a group of Vikings led by Erik the Red established two colonies on Greenland. These Viking settlements survived until about 1500.

ROSS EXPEDITION

This picture shows British explorers John Ross and William Parry meeting with the Inuit of northwest Greenland in August 1818. A powerful female shaman had predicted the arrival of strange men in huge boats with "white wings"– actually sailing ships.

LEARNING FROM THE ARCTIC PEOPLES

In 1909, US explorer Robert Peary became the first man to reach the North Pole, helped by teams of Inuit. Peary wore snowshoes and Inuit-style clothing and used huskies to pull sledges in the same way as the Inuit. Many early European explorers died in the Arctic because they did not use the survival techniques developed by Arctic dwellers. Later expeditions drew on local peoples' experience and were more successful.

WHALE PRODUCTS

European countries found many uses for the whales they killed. Oil from whale blubber was burned to provide light and heat and also made into soap. Whale oil was used in many foods, including ice cream and margarine. Tough, springy baleen was made into many different products, including brushes, umbrellas, corsets and fishing rods.

soap

margarine

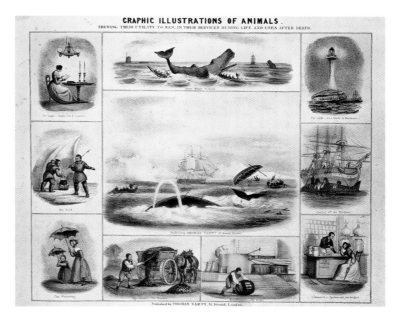

HUNTING THE WHALE

The illustration in the centre of this picture shows an early European whale hunt. Small open hunting boats were launched from a larger ship. Around the main picture, some of the ways in which the whales were used are shown. Europeans saw the whale as an extremely valuable resource.

WHALEBONE CORSET

This picture is taken from a catalogue dating back to the early 1900s. It shows a woman wearing a fashionable corset. Women wore these tight undergarments to keep their figures in shape. Corsets were strengthened with bony plates called baleen, which came from the mouths of whales. Baleen was also known as whalebone.

Trappers and Traders

THE WHALING INDUSTRY boomed during the 1700s. By 1800, however, the Europeans had slaughtered so many whales that these great creatures faced extinction, and some Arctic groups lost a valuable source of food. As the whaling industry declined, so the European settlers looked for new ways to profit from the region. Merchants soon realized that the soft, warm fur of Arctic mammals, such as sea otters and Arctic foxes, would fetch a high price in Europe. They began to trade with local hunters for these skins, setting up trading posts across the Arctic. In every region, the fur trade was controlled by the nation that had explored there first. Russia controlled all trade rights in Alaska. A British business called the Hudson Bay Trading Company controlled business in Canada.

Arctic people came to rely on the Europeans for metal tools and weapons. Soon, many Arctic people abandoned their traditional life of hunting. Instead, they trapped mammals for their skins and sold them to the merchants. Arctic people entered troubled times. Diseases previously unknown in the region, such as measles and tuberculosis, killed thousands of men, women and children.

SKINS FOR SALE
The skins of seals and Arctic foxes hang in a store in northwest Greenland. During the 1800s and early 1900s, otter, fox and mink fur became extremely popular in Europe. European merchants made huge profits from the trade but paid Arctic hunters low rates for trapping these valuable animals.

CONVENIENCE FOOD
In 1823 this tin of veal was prepared for Sir William Parry's expedition to the Arctic. European explorers, whalers and traders introduced many foods to the native Arctic peoples. Local trappers exchanged furs for food and other goods. However, the result was that some Arctic people began to rely on the food provided by the traders rather than hunting for their own food.

TRADING POST
This engraving, made around 1900, shows an Inuit hunter loading his sledge with European goods at a trading post in the far north of Canada. By the mid-1800s, fortified posts such as this had sprung up all over Arctic North America. The British Hudson Bay Trading Company, which was set up in the 1820s, became very wealthy exploiting Canada's natural resources.

ADDICTED TO ALCOHOL

Whisky was traded throughout the Arctic in the 1800s and 1900s. As well as goods made from metal, merchants introduced European foods and stimulants, such as tea, coffee, sugar, alcohol and tobacco, to the Arctic. Many Arctic hunters became addicted to spirits, such as whisky. This made them rely even more heavily on traders who could supply them with alcohol.

SCRIMSHAW

During the long Arctic nights or lengthy voyages across the ocean, European explorers, sailors and traders occupied their time carving pictures and patterns on whale bones and walrus tusks. This work was called scrimshaw. First, a design was scratched in the bone or tusk using a knife or needle. Then the artist made the picture visible by rubbing soot into the scratches.

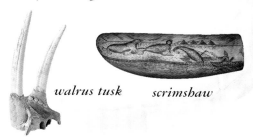

soot

walrus tusk   *scrimshaw*

POWERFUL WEAPON

This engraving shows a number of British rifles from the 1840s. During the 1800s and 1900s, European guns and rifles transformed traditional hunting methods in the Arctic. Rifles were much more accurate than the old Arctic weapons, bows and arrows, and could target prey from a much greater distance.

GOODS FOR TRADE

Local hunters trade with Europeans in a local store in this engraving. Hundreds of metal tools and weapons were traded by Europeans in the Arctic, most often for animal skins. European merchants also bartered rifles, saws, knives, drills, axes and needles. The Inuit and other Arctic groups soon came to depend on these valuable tools and weapons.

Cold-weather Clothing

I N THE BITTERLY COLD WINDS and snowstorms, Arctic people needed warm, waterproof clothing to survive. They used animal skins to insulate them from the harsh conditions. Two layers of skins were worn – a tough outer layer with the fur facing outwards and soft, warm underclothes with the fur facing inwards. The fur of the underclothes trapped a layer of warm air next to the person's skin, thus maintaining a constant body temperature. Only a tiny part of a person's body was left exposed to the freezing air.

Outer garments included hooded coats made from reindeer skin, trousers made from the hide of polar bears, and deer- or sealskin boots. When hunting in *kayaks,* Inuit men often wore waterproof *anoraks* (an Inuit word) made from thin strips of seal intestine sewn together. Underclothes included seabird-skin vests and socks made from the skins of reindeer calves.

FUR COAT
This girl is wearing a *yagushka*, the traditional jacket worn by Nenet women. The girl's mother has used dark strips of reindeer skin to decorate the jacket. Mittens and a fur-trimmed hood provide extra protection against the icy winds.

GRASS-LINED BOOTS
A Saami herder lines his reindeer-skin boots with dried grass. Hay provided a soft padding and also trapped a layer of air inside the boots to protect the herder's feet against the bitter cold.

MAKE SOME MITTENS
You will need: 4 pieces of shammy leather, black marker, scissors, PVA glue, glue brush, ruler, light blue and red felt, black pen.

1 Draw around your hand on a piece of shammy leather, leaving a 1.5 cm gap around your hand shape. You will need two pieces of leather per hand.

2 Glue around the edge of the right-hand glove and glue a left-hand glove into position. Repeat this with the other two glove shapes. Leave them to dry.

3 Cut out two pieces of shammy leather, each approximately 20 x 5 cm. Cut a 2 cm fringe on the edge of each piece of shammy leather.

PREPARING SKINS

This Inuit woman is chewing a piece of sealskin to soften it. She uses her front teeth so the skin does not get too wet. In the past, the teeth of old women were worn right down by years of chewing skins. The skin of a bearded seal was used to make the soles of sealskin boots, because it was waterproof and gripped the ice well.

SEWING MATERIALS

Arctic women made all their family's clothes by hand. Bone or antler needles were shaved to a fine point, then rubbed smooth on stones so they did not snag or tear the animal skins. Whale or reindeer sinew was used as thread. When wet, the sinew swelled slightly to make the seams waterproof. Today, Arctic women sew with fine steel needles and use dental floss as thread. Cotton wool is now used to line boots instead of grass.

cotton wool *dental floss*

grasses

DRESSED IN SKINS

Inuit hunters wore warm jackets, such as this parka, as well as leggings made from reindeer hide and *kamik*, or sealskin, boots. The warm hood of the jacket helped to preserve body heat. Hoods were often trimmed with wolf or wolverine hair, because these furs shed the ice that formed as the person breathed.

NEEDLE CASE

This needle case is made from reindeer bone and hide. It would have been worn on the belt of a Saami woman. The needles it held were made from slivers of bone, walrus tusk or antler. Needles were very important to Arctic people. Hand-sewn clothes and bedding took many hours to make and often needed repairs to keep the items warm and waterproof.

Rather than gloves, people of the Arctic wore fingerless mittens to keep their hands warm. Children's mittens were sometimes sewn into the sleeves of their parka to stop them from getting lost. Some mittens were embroidered with decorative patterns.

4 Glue along the edge of the fringe shammy and position it around the wrist area of one of the mittens. Make sure the fringe faces forwards.

5 Use a black marker to draw six blue flower shapes (about 5 cm in diameter) and six red circles (about 8 mm in diameter). Cut these shapes out.

6 Glue the red dots you have made to the centre of each blue flower. Repeat this procedure for all six blue flowers and wait for the glue to dry.

7 Decorate the back of the mittens with the flowers. Cut two flowers in half for the wrists and draw in the leaves and stalks with a black pen.

Costumes and Ornaments

ARCTIC CLOTHES were often beautiful as well as practical. Strips or patches of different furs were used to form designs and geometric patterns on outer clothes. Fur trimmings, toggles and other decorative fastenings added the final touches to many clothes. Jewellery included pendants, bracelets, necklaces and brooches. These ornaments were traditionally made of natural materials, such as bone and walrus ivory.

In North America, Inuit women often decorated clothes with birds' beaks, tiny feathers or even porcupine quills. In Greenland, lace and glass beads were popular decorations. Saami clothes were the most colourful in the Arctic. Saami men, women and children wore blue outfits with a bright red and yellow trim. Mens' costumes included a tall hat and a short flared tunic. Womens' clothes included flared skirts with embroidered hems and colourful hats, shawls and scarves.

SAAMI COSTUME

A Saami man wears the traditional costume of his region, including a flared tunic trimmed with bright woven ribbon at the neck, shoulders, cuffs and hem. Outfits such as the one above were worn all year round. In winter, Saami people wore thick fur parkas, called *peskes,* over the bright tunics.

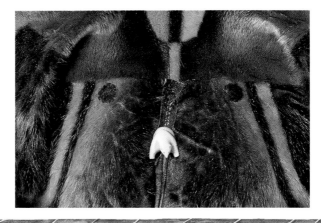

BEAR TOGGLE

An ivory toggle carved into the shape of a polar bear completes this traditional sealskin jacket. Arctic people took great pride in their appearance and loved to decorate their clothes in this way. In ancient times, the Inuit, for example, decorated their garments with hundreds of tiny feathers or the claws of mammals, such as foxes or hares. Women often decorated all the family's clothes.

MAKE A SAAMI HAT

You will need: red felt (58 x 30 cm), PVA glue, glue brush, black ribbon (58 x 2 cm), coloured ribbon, white felt, ruler, pencil, compass, red card, scissors, red, green and white ribbon (3 at 44 x 4 cm), red ribbon (58 x 4 cm).

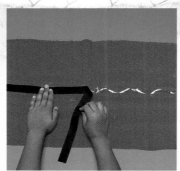

1 Mark out the centre of the red felt along its length. Carefully glue the length of black ribbon along the centre line, as shown above.

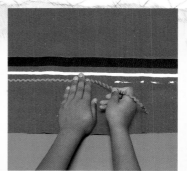

2 Continue to decorate the felt with different kinds of coloured ribbon and white felt, making a series of strips along the red felt, as shown above.

3 Cut out a circle of red card with a diameter of 18 cm. Draw a circle inside with a diameter of 15 cm. Cut into the larger circle to the 15 cm line.

CURVING BOOT

This picture shows a curved boot worn by the Saami people from Arctic Scandinavia. These boots are designed for use with skis and are decorated with traditional woollen pompoms. The curved boot tips stop the skier from slipping out of the skis when travelling uphill.

WEDDING FINERY

The bride, bridegroom and a guest at a Saami wedding in north Norway all wear the traditional outfits. Notice that the style of the man's wedding hat differs from the one shown in the picture on the opposite page. Both men and women wear brooches encrusted with metal disks. Saami women's wedding outfits include tall hats, tasselled shawls and ribbons.

BEADS AND LACE

A woman from western Greenland wears the traditional beaded costume of her nation, which includes a top with a wide black collar and cuffs and high sealskin boots. After European settlers arrived in Greenland, glass beads and lace became traditional decorations on clothing. Hundreds of beads were sewn onto jackets to make intricate patterns.

The style of Saami hats varied from region to region. In southern Norway, men's hats were tall and rounded. Further north, their hats had four points.

4 Glue the ends of the decorated red felt together, as shown above. You will need to find the right size to fit around your head.

5 Fold down the tabs cut into the red card circle. Glue the tabs, then stick the card circle to the felt inside one end of the hat.

6 While the hat is drying, glue the coloured ribbon strips together. Glue these strips 15 cm from the end of the 58 cm long red ribbon band.

7 Glue the 58 cm band of red ribbon onto the base of the hat, making sure the shorter strips of red, green and white ribbons go over the top of the band.

Arts and Crafts

ARCTIC PEOPLE were accomplished artists. Tools, weapons and ornaments were all made by hand. Across the Arctic, men and women were skilled at carving, sewing, leather-work, basket-making, beadwork and, in some areas, metal-working. In ancient times, objects were always made to be as useful as possible and were not seen as works of art. Today, however, tools and ornaments made by Arctic craftspeople are prized as works of art and fetch high prices when they are sold around the world.

Carving was one of the most important arts in the Arctic, but carving materials were always scarce. Artists engraved designs on bone and ivory, and they carved stone, bone, ivory and reindeer antler into tools and sculptures. Carving tools included knives, needles and bow drills. Some carvings were polished using natural abrasives, such as sand, stone and rough animal skin.

FINE CARVING
This Inuit soapstone carving shows a hunter with his harpoon at the ready. Arctic carvings traditionally featured animals and birds of the region, scenes from everyday life and figures from myths and legends. They were made using knives, needles and bow drills.

MALE AND FEMALE ARTISTS
This early photograph, taken in 1900, shows an Inuit hunter using a bow drill to carve a piece of ivory. His wife makes a pair of *mukluks,* or deerskin boots. Today, Inuit sculptors use electrical power tools as well as knives and hand-drills for carving.

INUIT CARVING
You will need: a bar of soap (about 10 x 7 cm), dark coloured felt-tip pen, a metal nail file.

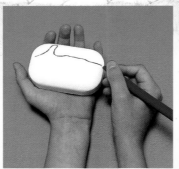

1 First wash your hands so that the bar of soap does not get marked. Draw out the basic shape of a dog on the bar of soap using your felt-tip pen.

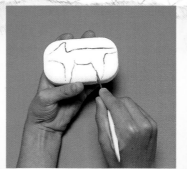

2 Begin the carving by cutting away the excess areas of soap around the shape you have drawn. Always make sure you cut away from your hand.

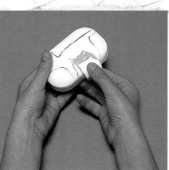

3 Carefully cut away the largest areas of the soap first, as shown above. Make sure the soap does not crumble as you break the pieces away.

SOAPSTONE POTS

Pots and other containers were sometimes made from soapstone (steatite) in the Arctic. This stone is soft enough to carve and hollow out. Knives and bow drills were used as carving tools. People often made long trips by dogsled to collect the stone from the places in which it was found.

soapstone

HAND-CRAFTED TOOLS

This cup and knife were crafted by Saami artists. The cover of the long knife is made from the antler of a reindeer and has been engraved with a decorative pattern. The handle is covered with leather. The drinking cup is carved from a piece of wood. You can just see the small piece of reindeer antler set into the handle of the cup.

PRINT-MAKING

An artist from Holman Island in the Canadian Arctic works on her print, dabbing paint through a stencil using a short, stubby brush. Print-making is a relatively new craft in the Arctic, but many of the subjects chosen are traditional.

SKILLFUL STITCHERS

This picture shows a wall hanging from an Inuit church in Canada. Arctic women were skilled sewers. Many clothes and items such as blankets are now considered works of art.

In the Arctic, carving is a skill that dates back thousands of years. Weapons, tools and various ornaments were carved from natural materials, such as bone, ivory, stone or driftwood.

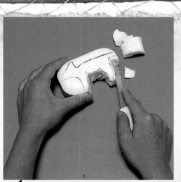

4 Carve away the smaller areas to make the shape more detailed. You should see the basic shape of the dog appear. Continue to carve the soap slowly.

5 Once you have cut out the basic shape of the dog, gradually and gently smooth the rough edges away. The legs and tail will be particularly fragile.

6 Continue to shape the smaller areas to give the dog carving more detail around the ears, legs, tail, stomach, neck and snout.

7 Finally, carefully carve out the smaller features of the head, such as the mouth and the eyes. Flatten the feet so the dog can stand on its legs.

Beliefs and Rituals

Long before Christian missionaries arrived in the Arctic, local people had developed their own beliefs. Arctic people thought that all living creatures possessed a spirit or *inua*. When an animal died, its spirit lived on and was reborn in another creature. Powerful spirits were thought to control the natural world, and these invisible forces influenced people's everyday lives. Some spirits were believed to be friendly towards humans. Others were malevolent or harmful. People showed their respect for the spirits by obeying taboos – rules that surrounded every aspect of life. If a taboo was broken the spirits would be angered. People called shamans could communicate with the spirit world. Shamans had many different roles in the community. They performed rituals to bring good luck in hunting, predicted the weather and the movements of the reindeer herds and helped to heal the sick. They worked as doctors, priests and prophets, all rolled into one.

SHAMAN AND DRUM
An engraving from the early 1800s shows a female shaman from Siberia. Most, but not all, shamans were male. Shamans often sang and beat on special drums, such as the one shown above, to enter a trance. Some drums had symbols drawn on them and helped the shamans to predict the future.

TUPILAK CARVING
This little ivory carving from Greenland shows a monster called a *tupilak*. *Tupilaks* were evil spirits. If someone wished an enemy harm, he might secretly make a little carving similar to this, which would bring a real *tupilak* to life. It would destroy the enemy unless the person possessed even more powerful magic to ward it off.

SHAMAN'S DRUM

You will need: ruler, scissors, thick card, PVA glue, glue brush, masking tape, compass, pencil, shammy leather, brown paint, paint brush, water pot, brown thread or string

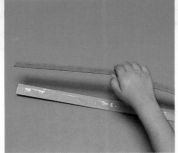

1 Cut out two strips of thick card, each strip measuring 77 cm long and 3 cm wide. Glue the two strips together to give the card extra thickness.

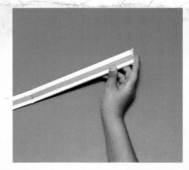

2 Once the glue has dried, use masking tape to cover the edges of the double-thickness card. Try to make the edges as neat as possible.

3 Using a compass, draw a circle with a 24 cm diameter on a piece of shammy leather. Cut it out, leaving a 2 cm strip around the edge of the circle.

HERBAL MEDICINES

An Innu woman collects pitcher plants that she will use to make herbal medicines. In ancient times, shamans acted as community doctors. They made medicines from plants and gave them to sick people to heal them. They also entered trances to soothe angry spirits, which helped the sick to recover from their illness.

SEA SPIRIT

This beautiful Inuit sculpture shows a powerful spirit called Sedna. The Inuit believed that Sedna controlled storms and all sea creatures. If anyone offended Sedna, she withheld her blessing and hunting was poor. Here Sedna is portrayed with a mermaid's tail and accompanied by a narwhal and two seals. This very delicate carving has been made from a piece of reindeer antler.

MAGIC MASK

This mask is from Arctic North America. It was worn by Inuit shamans during a special ritual to communicate with the spirit world. Shamans wore wooden masks similar to this one. They also wore head-dresses. Each mask represented a powerful spirit. The shaman would call on the spirit by chanting, dancing and beating on a special drum.

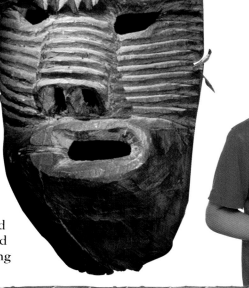

Shamans' drums were made of deerskin stretched over a round wooden frame. The shaman sometimes drew pictures of people, animals and stars on the side of the drum.

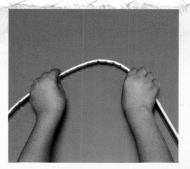

4 Using your fingers, curve the strip of card, as shown above. Make sure you curve the card slowly so that it does not crease.

5 Glue the card onto the circle. Ask someone to help keep the shammy leather stretched as you go. Tape the ends of the card together.

6 Make cuts 3 cm apart along the edge of the excess shammy leather towards the card, as shown above. Glue the edges to the cardboard ring.

7 Paint the card with dark brown paint and leave it to dry. Decorate the drum with thick brown thread or string by tying it around the edges.

The Long Polar Night

Winter lasts for many months in the Arctic. Communities living in the far north experience nearly three months of darkness in winter, because the Sun never rises above the horizon. During the long, dark days and nights, ancient peoples gathered round the fire to keep warm. The men still went out hunting so their families could eat, but there were many days when bad weather kept them in the camp. During this time, the family came together and listened to stories, sang, laughed and swapped jokes. The older people told myths and legends that had been passed down for generations. These stories explained the existence of the heavens or told how people and animals came to live in the Arctic. Adults practiced crafts and taught their children new skills. Men carved tools and fixed their hunting equipment, while women repaired the family's clothes and bedding. Winter was also a time for making ornaments, such as bracelets and brooches. Children practiced with string puzzles and played traditional games such as *ajagaq*.

SAAMI SONG
This Saami man is singing a traditional song called a *joik* (pronounced yoik). These light-hearted songs were made up on the spot, and there were no instruments to accompany the singer. These songs told the story of the day's events but used nonsense words and puns. Often, they poked fun at friends and family.

SINGING AND DRUMMING
Four young men perform a traditional drum-song in the Northwest Territories of Canada. Music provided entertainment during long Arctic evenings. Families sang and beat on skin drums with sticks of bone or reindeer antler.

MAKE A BROOCH

You will need: ruler, compass, pencil, thin card, scissors, PVA glue, glue brush, large button, aluminium foil, small roll of sticky tape, small nail varnish bottle, masking tape, safety pin.

1 Using the ruler, set your compass to draw a circle with a diameter of 8 cm on the thin card. Mark the circle lightly in pencil.

2 Cut the 8 cm circle out with your pair of scissors. When using scissors, always make sure that you cut away from your body.

3 Carefully glue the large button to the centre of the card circle. The compass point will have marked out the centre of the circle for you.

MYTHS AND LEGENDS

In the story illustrated to the right, a young Inuit called Taligvak uses magic to catch a seal at a time when other hunters in his village are finding it impossible to catch food. During the long Arctic winter, young children listened to stories like these told by their parents and grandparents. In this way, traditional legends passed down the generations.

The Saami of Lapland used beautiful brooches to fasten their jackets and shawls.

A TIME FOR CRAFTS

Beadwork is a traditional craft in Siberia. The Arctic winter was a good time to practice all kinds of crafts and to repair equipment. Men mended fishing nets and harpoons, while the women stitched new clothes and bedding and repaired garments that had got torn.

4 Cover the front of the card and the button with aluminium foil. Fold the edge over onto the back of the card circle and secure it with glue.

5 Draw around the inside of a small roll of sticky tape on a piece of foil. Repeat this 24 times. Cut out the silver foil circles with your scissors.

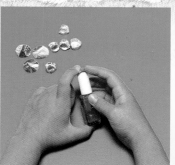

6 Place each foil circle over the lid of the nail varnish bottle, and carefully mould the edges over the lid to make 24 small discs.

7 Glue the discs onto the brooch, starting from the middle and working out. Tape a safety pin to the back of the brooch to make a fastening.

Ceremonies and Festivals

ARCTIC CEREMONIES were important occasions. If somebody died, a ceremony was performed to honour that person. In Inuit society, if someone died in an igloo a hole was cut in the wall of the igloo to carry the dead person out. The body was then sewn into a skin bag and laid out on the ground to face the rising Sun. Finally, the body was buried under a mound of stones. The Chukchi of Siberia believed that when a person died, their spirit went to live in the camps of the "Realm of the Polar Star". People were laid to rest with prize possessions that would help them in the afterlife. A great seamstress would be buried with her needles, thread and thimbles. A hunter was buried with his favourite weapons.

People also came together for festivals during the Arctic year. Spring drum ceremonies celebrated the return of the light and the approaching time of plenty. People met to feast, gossip, dance and sing. Other ceremonies gave thanks for the season's hunting. At festivals throughout the Arctic, people showed off their strength and skills in sports contests. Sports included seal skinning, wrestling, dog and reindeer racing and blanket tossing.

TUG OF WAR
Two Inuit boys compete in a tug of war. This traditional sport tested the strength of both young and old. Opponents tugged on wooden handles bound by a stout strip of sealskin, as shown above. Other tests of strength included the painful sports of finger-wrestling and cheek-pulling.

SEAL SKINNING
An Inuit woman works fast to skin a seal in record time at a skinning contest held in northwest Canada. Contestants often used their teeth to grip the skin while both hands were busy with the *ulu,* or rounded skinning knife.

RACING REINDEER
A herder urges on his reindeer team during a race in Siberia. Reindeer and dog races were traditional at Arctic festivals. Hunters enjoyed the chance to show off their well-trained teams. Light sledges were used so the animals could run as fast as possible. Reindeer racing is still a popular sport in some parts of the Arctic.

WRESTLING CONTEST

Two Nenet men wrestle during a spring festival on the tundra of the Yamal Peninsula in Siberia. Wrestling is a popular sport in many parts of the Arctic. It allows men to show off their strength and skill. The winner must throw his opponent to the ground.

HIGH KICK

This picture shows high kick being played in a modern gym. The high kick is a traditional Inuit sport. Contestants have to kick the ball with one part of their body still in contact with the ground. Traditionally, the ball was an inflated seal bladder hung on a hide string.

BLANKET TOSSING

A carving from Siberia shows a family playing the traditional Arctic sport of blanket-tossing. Boys and girls were tossed high in the air and caught in a strong, springy blanket made from animal hide. Adults held the blanket tightly or gripped hide cords sewn into the blanket's edge.

DOG-SLEDGE RACING

A team of huskies strain as they pull a sledge along a course in Finland. Dog racing was a competitive sport in the Arctic. Owners valued their dogs highly. Winning a race was a sign of a healthy pack. Dog teams were well looked after and given extra food before a big race.

Development of the Arctic

PANNING FOR GOLD
An early photograph shows a prospector panning for gold in a stream in the Klondike region of Alaska. Russia sold Alaska to the United States in 1867. In the late 1800s, gold was discovered there, and many new settlers rushed to the region to get rich quick.

DURING THE LATE 1800s, gold was discovered in the Yukon and at Klondike in the North American subarctic. A gold rush began, and thousands of prospectors flooded into the region to make their fortune. Many new settlements were founded on the tundra. In the wake of the new settlers, Christian missionaries arrived. They built schools and churches and worked to convert the local people to Christianity. Traditional ways of life in the Arctic began to vanish forever.

By 1900, all of the Arctic was owned by countries such as the United States, Canada and Russia, whose capitals lay much farther to the south. Greenland became part of Denmark, and Lapland was divided between Norway, Sweden, Finland and Russia. The governments of these nations cared little about local peoples. They were mainly interested in exploiting the minerals and other riches of the Arctic. Police posts were set up, and southern laws and traditions were imposed. Around the time of World War II (1939–1945), southern governments became interested in the Arctic for military purposes. Army radar bases sprang up throughout the region. Gradually, some of these bases became new towns.

GOLD MINING IN SIBERIA
This picture shows a modern gold mine near the town of Bilibino in the mountains of eastern Siberia. Gold was discovered in Siberia around the same time as the famous gold rush in North America. Soon diamonds, platinum, coal and other valuable minerals and metals were also mined in Arctic Russia. The exploitation of Siberia's natural resources had a devastating effect on the local people. The new mines scarred the countryside and took over lands where Siberian herders had lived for centuries.

COMMUNIST RUSSIA

This picture shows a Nenet work brigade during the spring migration of the reindeer. Following the Russian Revolution in 1917, the Soviet Union took power in Russia and the communist system was imposed in Siberia. Nenet, Chukchi and other herders were divided into Soviet brigades and sent to work on state farms and in industry. Traditional reindeer pastures were taken over by oil companies and other state businesses.

MILITARY BASES

This photograph shows a Distance Early Warning (DEW) radar station in Alaska. After World War II ended in 1945, a time of hostility between the United States and Russia known as the Cold War began. The Americans set up a line of DEW radar stations across the Arctic to warn of an impending Soviet attack, and the Soviets set up similar bases in Siberia. New towns grew up around some stations as the threat of war receded.

MINING TOWN

An early photograph taken in 1898 shows hundreds of people flocking to a newly opened drug store in Dawson City in the Klondike. As more and more gold prospectors arrived in the Arctic, the early ramshackle communities of miners' huts grew into major towns, such as Dawson City, each with southern laws and traditions.

CHRISTIANITY IN THE ARCTIC

The Dean of north Greenland stands outside Zion's Church in Illulissat. In the 1800s and early 1900s, Christian missionaries arrived in the Arctic in increasing numbers. They discouraged the work of the shamans and undermined local peoples' faith in the spirit world. Although Christianity helped to destroy traditional Arctic beliefs and customs, many Arctic people embraced Christianity, and it remains the most popular religion today.

Learning and Change

B Y THE MID-1900s, the lives of some Arctic people had been affected by mining and other activities in the region. However, the issue of children's education brought about the biggest changes of all. In the past, Arctic children had learned traditional skills from their parents at home or as they travelled from place to place. Now, governments in the south decided that Arctic children should get a formal education from paid teachers at school.

In North America, Inuit boys and girls began to attend schools in local towns. Parents moved there too and, for the first time, settled down to be near their children. In Siberia and Scandinavia, many children were sent to boarding schools far from their parents. At school, children learned new subjects and grew up with very different values to their parents. They turned away from the old life of hunting and herding, and many of the old Arctic skills and customs were lost.

SOUTHERN VALUES

Two Inuit boys play at cowboys using "guns" made from the jawbones of reindeer. For most of the 20th century, Arctic children learned more about the history and culture of nations such as the United States and Russia, than they did about their own culture. As a result, the traditional customs of Arctic people were undermined and lost.

KAYAK BUILDING

Inuit women teach the young wife of a hunter to sew sealskin onto a *kayak* frame, using a method that has been used for hundreds of years. Nowadays, many young Arctic people want to learn more about their ancestors. All over the Arctic, people are now being encouraged to take an interest in reviving the traditional skills of their predecessors.

SYLLABIC SYSTEM

This illustration shows the syllabic language system used by the Inuit in the Arctic. It was invented by Christian missionaries. Traditionally, Arctic languages were never written down. Each symbol represents a sound rather than a single letter. This makes it more difficult to use than alphabetic script.

LANGUAGE AND TEACHING

Inuit children work at a computer in a school in northern Canada. The words on the screen are written in syllabics. For most of the 20th century, children learned their lessons in languages such as English, Swedish and Russian. By the time they returned home, they had forgotten much of their own language and could hardly talk to their parents.

TRADITIONAL SKILLS

Two Inuit boys learn to build a sledge at school in northwest Greenland. For many years, the old skills of Arctic groups were not taught in schools. Recently, however, Arctic people have taken a new pride in their culture. Sledge-building and sewing lessons are now part of the curriculum at many schools.

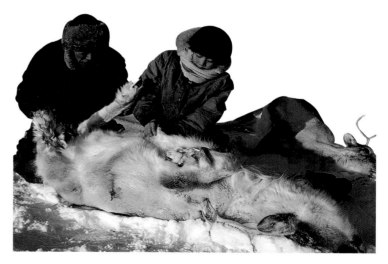

HUNTING TRIP

A young Inuit boy and his father skin a reindeer they have killed on a hunting expedition. For much of the 20th century, traditional skills, such as hunting, skinning and herding, were no longer considered important. Recently, however, they have been revived. The school system has been improved, and in many schools boys are now given time off to go on hunting trips.

The Arctic Today

During the second half of the 20th century, mining continued to accelerate in the Arctic. In 1968, vast deposits of oil and gas were found at Prudhoe Bay in Alaska. Mining caused pollution and disturbed traditional ways of life. In the 1980s, there were several major disasters. The giant oil spill from the supertanker *Exxon Valdez* polluted a huge area of the Alaskan coastline, killing many plants and animals. In 1986, the Chernobyl nuclear power station in the Ukraine caught fire and released a cloud of radioactive gas. The radiation poisoned the feeding grounds of the reindeer in Lapland – a disaster for the Saami herders.

From the 1970s, Arctic groups began to organize their own response to development in the region. They laid claim to lands where their ancestors had hunted and herded for centuries. In recent years, Arctic groups have won many major land claims. In 1990, the Inuit gained a large homeland in northern Canada, which they named Nunavut. It was handed over in 1999. Today, Arctic groups take a new pride in their heritage, and lost skills are being revived.

OLD AND NEW

A Saami rides a modern snowmobile across a frozen lake in Finland. In the past, Saami herders used reindeer to pull sledges across the frozen Arctic landscape. For most Arctic people, however, life today is a mix of ancient and modern ways. The Inuit, Saami and many other Arctic groups use the new technologies of the developed world while holding onto the traditions and culture of their ancestors.

OIL MINING IN ALASKA

The Trans-Alaskan pipeline snakes for thousands of miles across the Arctic tundra, carrying oil mined at Prudhoe Bay in northern Alaska south to the ice-free port of Valdez. From there, the oil is shipped all over the world in giant supertankers. Unfortunately, the Trans-Alaskan pipeline cuts across traditional Inuit hunting grounds and caribou migration routes which have been used by the deer for thousands of years. The Trans-Alaskan pipeline is just one example of how development and industry in the Arctic has disturbed the traditional way of life in the region.

OIL SPILL

A cormorant whose feathers are clogged with oil from the *Exxon Valdez* disaster lies dead on the coast of Alaska. In 1989, the oil tanker *Exxon Valdez* struck a reef in Alaskan waters. Thousands of tonnes of oil were spilled into the sea. Alaskan coasts were polluted with the oil as it washed ashore, and thousands of sea otters, seabirds and other creatures died.

PROTEST GROUPS

Bulldozers clear the site of a new dam in 1979 whilst protesters look on in horror. Between 1979 and 1981, the Saami organized a major protest against plans to build a dam on the River Alta in Norway. Unfortunately, the protest was unsuccessful – the campaigners lost the battle to prevent construction in the courts. Peaceful protest is an essential part of a democratic society. People can get their views heard through campaigns such as these. They may even be able to influence the outcome of controversial plans.

OUR LAND

In 1999, Inuit and other Arctic groups celebrated as the large homeland of Nunavut in northern Canada was handed over to them. The name *Nunavut* means "our land" in the Inuit language. The territory is the size of Norway. Nunavut is just one of a number of land claims that have been settled in recent years. Arctic groups have also won a share in profits from mining and industrial operations conducted on their lands.

POWER OF THE PEOPLE

Young people who live in the Arctic have much to look forward to in the future. Computers and communications allow them to overcome the problems of distance and be in touch with people around the world. They can share their pride in their culture and their unique environment with visitors and also via the Internet. By the time this boy has grown up, he will be a citizen of the world, not just of the Arctic.

Glossary

A

Ajagaq An ancient spear game played by children in the Arctic.
Amaut Back pouch used to carry Inuit babies and young children.
Anorak An Inuit word meaning an outer jacket.
Archaeologist A scientist who studies the past.
Arctic The region in the far north of our planet, surrounding the North Pole.
Arctic Circle An imaginary line circling the earth at a latitude of 66° 33' North that marks the limit of the Arctic. All areas inside the Arctic Circle experience at least one day a year when the sun never sets, and one day on which it never rises.

B

Baleen The horny plates which hang down inside the mouths of some whales and which are used to filter small sea creatures, the whale's food, from the water.
Beluga A small, white-skinned Arctic whale.
Blizzard A strong wind that blows at the same time as a heavy snowfall.
Blubber A layer of fat found under the skin of seals, whales and walruses, which helps them keep warm in icy water.
Bow drill Ancient tool used to start a fire by creating heat.

C

Cache To hide a store of food, or the food store itself.
Caribou A wild reindeer native to the Arctic.
Chukchi A reindeer-herding people of northeastern Siberia.
Cold War A time of hostility between the West and the Soviet Union. It followed World War II and lasted until the 1980s.
Continent Name for the large areas of land that cover the Earth. The continents are Antarctica, North and South America, Asia, Africa, Australia and Europe.

D

Distance Early Warning (DEW) A line of radar stations that were built across the American Arctic.
Drag handle Tool that is used to haul animal carcasses across the ice and snow.
Evenk A once-nomadic people of eastern Siberia.

F

Floe A floating sheet of sea-ice.
Fiord Narrow coastal inlet found in Scandinavia, where the land falls steeply to the sea.

H

Harpoon A spear-like weapon attahed to a long line that is used to catch whales and seals.

I

Ice Age One of a number of times in the Earth's history when large parts of the planet surface became covered with ice.
Iceberg An enormous chunk of ice that floats in the sea.
Ice cap A mass of ice that permanently covers land in the polar regions. Greenland has the largest ice cap in the Arctic.
Igloo An Inuit word meaning house, often used to refer to Inuit shelters built of ice blocks.
Inua An Inuit word that means spirit.
Inuit An ancient people of the American Arctic. The name simply means "the people".
Inukshuk A stone column made by Inuit hunters, used to herd caribou into an ambush.
Ivory The hard, smooth, cream-coloured part of the tusks of elephants and walruses.

J

Joik Traditional Saami improvised songs that tell the story of the day's events.

K

Kakivak A three-pronged Inuit spear used to catch fish.
Kamik Sealskin boots.
Kapp *see* Saami
Kayak A one-person Inuit canoe powered by a double-

bladed paddle. The boat's wooden or bone frame is covered with sealskin.

L

Land bridge An area of dry land joining two land masses. In prehistoric times, a land bridge linked the continents of Asia and North America.

Latitude Imaginary lines that run parallel to the Equator of the Earth, going north and South. The Equator, running round the centre of the Earth, is 0°. The North Pole is 90°N and the South Pole is 90°S. Latitude is used by geographers to calculate the positions of places.

Lichen A living organism that grows on rocks in the Arctic and is eaten by caribou.

M

Mammal A type of warm-blooded animal such as human beings, whales, cats, and bats.

Migration A seasonal journey made by people or animals to find food or avoid extreme cold.

Missionary Someone who is sent by a religious organization to a foreign country to do religious and social work.

Mukluk Deerskin boots.

Muktuk A gristly layer found just below a whale's skin, eaten as a delicacy in the Arctic.

N

Narwhal A species of small Arctic whale.

Nenet A reindeer-herding people of western Siberia.

Nomad A person who continually moves from place to place to find food and water.

North Pole The most northerly point on the Earth.

Nunavut A large Inuit territory in northern Canada, established in 1999.

P

Pack ice Floating sea-ice.

Permafrost Permanently frozen ground. Permafrost can reach depths of 600 m in some areas.

Peske Thick fur parka worn by Saami people over their tunics.

Plankton Tiny plants and animals that drift around the surface of a sea or lake.

Prospector A person who searches for valuable minerals such as gold.

Pulkka A boat-shaped sleigh used in Siberia and Scandinavia.

S

Saami The ancient people of Lapland in Scandinavia.

Shaman A kind of priest thought to be able to contact the spirits and heal the sick.

Sinew The tissue that connects an animal's bones and muscles.

Slingshot Another name for a catapult.

Stallos People-eating monsters in Saami legends.

T

Taboo A rule or custom linked with religious beliefs that shows respect to the spirits.

Taiga A belt of forests found in the far north, south of the tundra.

Toboggan A wooden frame on runners used for sliding over snow and ice.

Tundra The barren, treeless lowlands of the far north.

U

Ulu A rounded knife used mostly by Inuit women to skin and cut meat.

Umiak An open boat, powered by oars and sometimes sails, used by the Inuit to hunt whales.

W

Whalebone *see* baleen

Wolverine A furry mammal that looks like a small bear, found in many of the northern forests of Europe, Asia and North America.

Y

Yagushka Traditional jacket worn by Nenet women.

Yakut A reindeer-herding people of northern Siberia.

Index